S0-ABZ-171

Gods, Goddesses, and Mythology

VOLUME 2

Ares–Celts

Marshall Cavendish
New York • London • Singapore

Marshall Cavendish
99 White Plains Road
Tarrytown, New York 10591

www.marshallcavendish.us

Library of Congress Cataloging-in-Publication Data

Gods, goddesses, and mythology/editor, C. Scott Littleton.
p. cm.
Includes bibliographical references and index.
ISBN 0-7614-7559-1 (set : alk. paper)
1. Mythology--Encyclopedias. I. Littleton, C. Scott. II. Marshall Cavendish Corporation. III. Title.

BL312.G64 2005
201'.3'03--dc22

2004040758

ISBN 0-7614-7559-1 (set)
ISBN 0-7614-7561-3 (vol. 2)

Printed and bound in China

09 08 07 06 05 6 5 4 3 2

General Editor
C. Scott Littleton, Occidental College, Los Angeles

Marshall Cavendish
Project Editor: Marian Armstrong
Editorial Director: Paul Bernabeo
Production Manager: Alan Tsai

Brown Reference Group
Project Editor: Chris King
Editors: Clive Carpenter, Deborah Evans, Lee Stacy
Designer: Steve Wilson
Picture Researcher: Helen Simm
Cartographer: Mark Walker
Indexer: Kay Ollerenshaw
Managing Editor: Tim Cooke

Picture Credits

Cover: Illustration of the story of Cadmus by Virginia Frances Sterrett. **Mary Evans Picture Library**

AKG: 168, 179, 272, S Domingie 173, Erich Lessing 150, 174, 175, 186, 244, 263, Gilles Mermet 232; **Art Archive:** Archaeological Museum, Amman, Jordan/Dagli Orti 163, British Museum, London 277, Chateau de Chambord/Dagli Orti 264, Musee Alesia Alise, Saint Reine, France/Dagli Orti 280, Musee d'Archeologie Mediterraneenne, Marseilles/Dagli Orti 286, Musee de la Civilisation Gallo-Romaine, Lyons/Dagli Orti 279, Museo Civico, Pavia/Dagli Orti 260, Museo Civico, Vicenza/Dagli Orti 156, National Anthropological Museum, Mexico/Dagli Orti 259, Ragab Papyrus Institute, Cairo/Dagli Orti 256; **Boston Museum of Fine Arts:** 185; **Bridgeman Art Library:** Archives Charmet 177, Hamburg Kunsthalle 169, Louvre, Paris 235, Louvre, Paris/Giraudon 164, 167, Manchester Art Gallery, UK 223, Musee des Beaux-Arts, Rouens, France/Giraudon 155, Museo Archeologico, Bari, Italy 236, Museo Archeologico Nazionale, Naples 157; **Corbis:** 258, Paul Almasy 269, 270, Archivo Iconografico SA 149, 261, Arte & Immagini srl 216, Yann Arthus-Bertrand 180, 182, Dave Bartuff 159, Niall Benvie 227, Bettmann 202, 238, 283, Bohemian Nomad Picturemakers 257, Christie's Images 218-219, Elio Ciol 210, L Clarke 201, Gianni Dagli Orti 162, 184, 204, 206, 208, 211, 213, 266, Araldo de Luca 154, Eric & David Hosking 197, Mimmo Jodice 148, 153, 172, 218, 275, Wolfgang Kaehler 225, Chris Rainier 196, Carmen Redondo 165, Roger Ressmeyer 200, Penny Tweedie 195, Vanni Archive 161, Rugero Vanni 170, Sandro Vannini 243, Roger Wood 188, 191, 268, 271, Adam Woolfitt 245; **Corbis Royalty Free:** 192-193; **Getty Images:** Photodisc 176, Image Bank 240, 249; **ICCE:** Marie Matthews 212; **Image State:** Ethel Davies 228; **Lebrecht Collection:** Interfoto, Munich 171, 246, 276; **Mary Evans Picture Library:** 217, 229, 252, 273, 282, 284; **Photos12.com:** ARJ 151, 152, Institut Ramses 255; **Scala Archives:** Museo Archeologico, Ferrera 274, Museo delle Ceramiche, Florence 251, Rovigo Pinacoteca dell'Accademia dei Concordi 265, Soprintendenza alle Antichi, Milano 187, E Stroudhal: 190; **Sylvia Cordaiy Photo Library:** Stephen Coyne 189, 222, Chris North 248; **Topham:** 166, 198, 199, 220, 221, 231, 250, 281, British Museum/HIP 158, 214, 285, Museum of London/HIP 237, Charles Walker 160, 181, 230, 254, 262; **Travel Ink:** William Gray 233; **World Art Kiosk:** California State University/Kathleen Cohen 215, CSULA Art Department 239; **Werner Forman Archive:** 241, Liverpool Museum 207, Museum fur Volkerkunde, Basel 209, National Museum of Anthropology, Mexico 205, Stofnun Arna Magnussonar a Islandi 234

CONTENTS

ARES

Strong, muscular, tall, and often cruel, Ares, the Greek god of war, was the most despised of all the Olympians. However, despite the low opinion the gods and the Greeks had of him, Ares did feature in two myths that provided enduring lessons in morality and honor. These were his love affair with the goddess Aphrodite and his alleged murder of Poseidon's son Halirrhothius.

Ares was the son of Zeus and Hera, the king and queen of the gods, although one version of Ares' birth has it that Hera conceived the god of war when she touched a flower. For the ancient Greeks, Ares was the personification of war, strife, and brute force. Despite his belligerence, he was often romantically involved, especially with Eos, goddess of the dawn, and Aphrodite, goddess of love, beauty, and marriage. Aphrodite was also the wife of Ares' crippled half brother Hephaestus, god of fire and metalworking.

The bloodthirsty god

References to Ares in Greek mythology depict him as always overeager for war and the first Olympian to join in a battle among mortals. In combat Ares usually wore a gleaming helmet and armor, carried a sword, and rode in a chariot. He was often accompanied by his

Left: The Ares Ludovisi *sculpture is a Roman copy of a Greek original. It is an unusually relaxed portrayal of the young war god.*

Above: Venus and Mars, Victory and Cupid *by the Italian painter Paris Bordone (1500–1571). Ares' Roman equivalent, Mars, was a popular subject for Renaissance artists.*

sister Eris, the goddess of strife; his sons Deimos, who symbolized fear and terror, and Phobos, who represented panic; and Enyo, a bloodthirsty war goddess. It was told that during a battle Ares would roam the field looking for the bloodiest fights to join, rarely caring on whose side he fought.

Many Greek myths describe Ares as despised by both mortals and most of the gods; even his own parents, Zeus and Hera, did not like him. In the *Iliad*, an epic poem by Homer (c. ninth-eighth century BCE), Zeus says to Ares, "Most hateful to me are you of all gods on Olympus, for ever is strife dear to you and wars and fighting."

Stories of Ares

Ares was the main character in very few Greek myths. However, he did play a small but significant role in many other myths and legends. In the story of Cadmus and the founding of Thebes, for example, the dragon that guarded the spring near where Cadmus was to build the new city was either the servant of Ares or an offspring. One version of the myth has it that for slaying the dragon Cadmus had to pay homage to Ares for eight years.

Hippolyte, the queen of the Amazons, was said to wear a belt, or girdle, that was a gift to her from Ares. The belt was meant to symbolize the queen's power, and the Greek hero Heracles successfully stole it from her as one of his 12 labors for the king Eurystheus. Another famous Greek legend involved the hero Jason, who, along with the Argonauts, went on an epic quest for the Golden Fleece. It hung in an oak grove in Colchis that was dedicated to Ares, guarded by a dragon that never slept. Jason was only able to obtain the fleece with the help of the sorceress Medea, who was the granddaughter of Helios the sun god.

Ares performed an unusual role in the myth of Sisyphus and Thanatos, god of death. After Sisyphus had told Asopus, a river god, that Zeus had stolen his daughter, Aegina, Zeus sent Thanatos to take Sisyphus away. In the underworld, however, Sisyphus tricked the god of death and tied him up. As long as Thanatos was unable to reach the land of the living, no one died on earth. This angered the gods, and they sent Ares to solve the problem.

Ares' first act was to release Thanatos. He then captured Sisyphus, who was still in the underworld, and delivered him to the god of death. Thinking he had solved the problem and pleased the other gods, Ares returned to Olympus, but Sisyphus tricked death again and ended up living to a ripe old age.

Ares in Sculpture and Painting

In art, Ares was depicted as a handsome, often youthful warrior. Most representations of him were sculptures rather than paintings, and in these he was usually shown wearing a helmet and holding a spear, shield, and sword. Sometimes he was even depicted wearing an aegis (a special goatskin cloak or breastplate honoring Zeus and Hera), but in literature and paintings it was his rival Athena who was more often associated with the aegis.

One of the most famous representations of Ares is a sculpture known as the Ares Borghese. The work, carved around 125 CE, acquired its name in the 18th century when it was purchased by a member of the Borghese family, a powerful Roman dynasty. It stands at over 6 feet (2 m) and shows the war god as young and nude, wearing nothing but his war helmet. Today the sculpture is housed in the Louvre in Paris.

Paintings of Ares are few, but the Roman equivalent, Mars, was a popular subject of many artists. Two of the many paintings of Mars show the god of war as young and handsome, highlighting the deity's virility. The exploits of Venus (Aphrodite) and Mars (Ares) inspired paintings such as Jacques-Louis David's *Mars Disarmed by Venus and the Graces* (c. 1824), which shows a mature god of war, draped in a bloodred cloak, lounging with Venus. *Mars and Venus Caught in the Net* (1536) by Maerten van Heemskerck shows the lovers trapped in Vulcan's (Hephaestus's) net, dragged before the gods.

Left: The Ares Borghese was carved in the second century CE, but historians believe it was based on a fifth-century-BCE Greek original.

Other views of Ares

Ares had some very contradictory characteristics. Depending on the myth, he could appear either strong or weak, stupid or intelligent, mean or noble, and immature or resolute. For example, he was too weak to stop the twin giants Ephialtes and Otus, who attacked Olympus in an attempt to overthrow Zeus. The giants tied up Ares in brass chains and forced him into a jar, where he stayed for 13 months before being rescued by Hermes, the messenger of the gods.

Ares' meaner nature was revealed in some versions of the story of the death of Adonis. Loved by the goddess Aphrodite, Adonis was a handsome mortal who had the bad luck to incur the jealousy of Ares. A few sources record that Ares, angry at Aphrodite's love for Adonis, transformed himself into the boar that gored Adonis to death.

Ares was also an amorous god. His many lovers included Aglaurus, who was either a nymph or an Athenian princess, and the goddesses Aphrodite and Eos. In one myth

Aphrodite grew so angry at Eos for making love to Ares that she cast a spell forcing Eos always to fall in love with someone new, never settling with one god or mortal.

In another myth Aphrodite's husband, Hephaestus, suspected that his wife was unfaithful. To catch her and her lover, he forged a metal net so thin it was invisible to all but Hephaestus, and so strong that not even the gods could break free of it. He placed the metal net around Aphrodite's bed to entrap whoever joined her there. Ares and Aphrodite were caught, and Hephaestus dragged them before the other gods, seeking justice for his betrayal and humiliation. However, the gods just roared with laughter at the two hapless lovers. Ares appeared wanton and foolish, incapable of extricating himself from the snare and from the ridicule of the gods.

The Trojan War

The Trojan War, the legendary conflict between the Greeks and the Trojans, was the subject of many myths in ancient Greece. In these myths all the gods used their respective powers to help or hinder either the Greeks or the Trojans. Accounts of his involvement in the Trojan War depict Ares as untrustworthy and immature. The god of war promised both Athena and Hera, queen of the gods, that he would side with the Greeks, but he broke his promise and sided with Aphrodite, who was aiding the Trojans. Hera and Athena vowed to punish Ares for his broken promise.

During the battle Ares was a fearsome sight. According to one source even the fierce Greek hero Diomedes shuddered at the sight of the bloodstained god and cried out to the Greek soldiers to retreat from the battlefield. It was then that Hera asked Zeus if she could drive Ares from the battlefield. Zeus agreed. Hera joined Diomedes in the battle and urged him to strike at Ares. Diomedes hurled his spear at the god of war. The spear was guided by the angry Athena, Ares' half sister, who was invisible even to the gods because she was wearing the Helmet of Hades. The injured Ares cried out loudly and rushed back to Olympus, where Paeon, god of healing, tended his wound.

After Paeon's treatment Ares returned to the battlefield outside the walls of Troy. Knowing that Athena had aided Diomedes, Ares attacked her. According to Homer, Athena was at first surprised that Ares would even attempt to challenge her, but she quickly shook off the attack and threw a giant boulder at Ares, knocking him to the ground.

Ares had been a bitter rival of Athena for many years before the start of the Trojan War. Whereas Ares relied on his brute force when fighting, Athena used skill, intelligence, and cunning to earn her victories. As a result,

Children of Ares

Ares had many children with goddesses, nymphs, and mortal women. His most famous son was Diomedes—not the Greek hero of the Trojan War, but the king of the Bistonians of Thrace and the owner of horses that ate human flesh. Heracles, the Greek hero famous for his 12 Labors, was charged with bringing the flesh-eating horses to Mycenae, but Diomedes refused to give up the animals, so Heracles fed the king to the horses. Heracles also killed another of Ares' sons, Cycnus. Cycnus challenged Heracles to a duel, but the Greek hero defeated him. During the battle Ares tried to intervene on the side of Cycnus, but Heracles wounded him as well as killing Cycnus.

Most of Ares' children were bloodthirsty and heartless, like their father, and several met violent deaths. Phlegyas, for example, had a daughter named Coronis. Coronis was seduced by Apollo, god of the sun and the arts. Phlegyas became so angry that he torched Apollo's temple at Delphi. In revenge Apollo sent Phlegyas to the underworld.

Below: This 1865 painting by Gustave Moreau (1826–1898) shows Ares' son Diomedes being attacked by flesh-eating horses.

Enyo and Bellona

Enyo was a Greek goddess of war and waster of cities, but she was a minor Olympian and had no extensive mythology of her own. She was most often depicted as the daughter of Ares, but occasionally as his mother or his sister. She was often described as covered in blood and looking violent. According to Homer, Enyo sided with Ares during the Trojan War, but when the city of Troy finally fell and the Trojans were slaughtered by the Greeks, Enyo danced herself into a frenzy "like a hurricane" at all the spilled blood. Enyo the war goddess should not be confused with Enyo of the Graeae. The Graeae were three old women, or crones, who were born with gray hair and were the sisters of the Gorgons; they were not related to Ares.

Enyo's Roman equivalent was Bellona, a goddess of war and a favorite of Roman soldiers. She was far more prominent in the Roman pantheon than Enyo was among the Greek gods. The Romans built a temple to Bellona in the Campus Martius ("field of Mars"), a place outside the gates of Rome. The Senate greeted foreign ambassadors at the temple. They also met with Roman generals there before they entered the city on their victory march known as the triumph.

Bellona was originally called Duellona, and some scholars believe that the Romans could have based her on an Etruscan deity whose characteristics were merged with those of the Greek Enyo. According to legend she accompanied Mars into battle, just as Enyo did with Ares, and was variously depicted as either Mars's wife, sister, or daughter. Artistic representations of Bellona usually have her holding a sword and wearing a helmet. She is also often armed with a spear and a torch.

Left: Peter Paul Rubens (1577–1640) painted a portrait of Marie de Médicis, queen of France, as the Roman goddess Bellona.

Athena was far more honored by the ancient Greeks than Ares. In further contrast, Athena never relished the prospect of war, but once the fighting started she devised a strategy that attempted to achieve a quick victory with minimal bloodshed. Away from the battlefield Athena missed no opportunity to humiliate Ares, whom she viewed as slow-witted. At the same time, just the sight of Athena sent Ares into a violent rage.

Origin and legacy

Some scholars believe that the concept of Ares did not originate in Greece but that the Greeks adopted him from Thracian mythology. Thrace was an ancient civilization that occupied the territory north of the Aegean Sea. Today Thrace forms a region that includes parts of Greece, Bulgaria, and Turkey. Both the ancient Greeks and Romans thought of Thrace (known as Thracia in Latin) as a country made up of fierce warriors. It is unclear whether the Thracian Ares was as battle-hungry and capricious as the Greek Ares, but in the Roman pantheon, Mars, who was modeled on Ares, was depicted as having more maturity and intelligence than the Greek deity.

Mars was originally an earth god and a god of spring, fertility, and growth. For some reason he eventually became associated with death and ultimately was viewed only as the Roman god of war. The Romans wrote far more positively of Mars than the Greeks did of Ares. In the *Aeneid*, an account of the founding of Rome by the poet Virgil (70–19 BCE), Roman warriors die gladly upon "Mars' field of renown." The soldiers worship Mars rather than fear and detest him. The Romans held festivals and built temples to honor him. With the significant exception of the Areopagus (Hill of Ares), located west of the Acropolis in Athens, the ancient Greeks barely acknowledged Ares in any public or tangible way. Other than the Areopagus, there was only one temple dedicated to Ares in all of Athens and only a single spring consecrated to him near Thebes.

***Right:** This Roman bust of Ares depicts a slightly older god of war than is usual. The Gorgon breastplate worn by this Ares was more commonly associated with Athena.*

A god on trial

The Areopagus was where criminal trials were held. It was named for Ares because, according to legend, he was the defendant in the first trial held there. When Halirrhothius, Poseidon's son, attempted to rape Alcippe, Ares' daughter by Aglaurus, Ares saw the attack and killed Halirrhothius. In retribution, Poseidon, god of the sea, demanded that Ares be tried for murder. At the Areopagus Ares pleaded his case before 12 Olympian gods who acquitted him.

Works by some of the major dramatists and writers of ancient Greece, including the playwright Euripides (c. 484–406 BCE), refer to this myth. Ares' trial on the Areopagus can be seen as a legal commentary about justifiable homicide. The 12 Olympian gods summed up their verdict by saying that it was wrong for Ares to have committed murder, but in this case the murder was justified because the god of war was defending his daughter's honor.

This was a rationale that would have resonated with the ancient Greeks, and similar kinds of justification have formed the basis for many legal decisions in the modern world. For instance, defendants on trial for murder are often acquitted if a jury can be persuaded to see the killing as morally justified. In ancient Greek and many modern Western courts, such justifications could include self-defense, the defense of property, or the defense of loved ones. It is perhaps ironic that a character as loathsome as Ares could stand for a legal code so commonly recognized.

ALYS CAVINESS

Bibliography

Bulfinch, Thomas. *Bulfinch's Mythology.* New York: Modern Library, 1998.

Graves, Robert. *The Greek Myths.* New York: Penguin USA, 1993.

Hamilton, Edith. *Mythology.* Boston, MA: Black Bay Books, 1998.

Homer, and Robert Fagles, trans. *The Iliad.* New York: Penguin USA, 2003.

Howatson, M. C., and Ian Chilvers. *Concise Oxford Companion to Classical Literature.* New York: Oxford University Press, 1993.

SEE ALSO: Adonis; Amazons; Aphrodite; Athena; Cadmus; Diomedes; Eos; Hephaestus; Hera; Heracles; Hermes; Mars; Paeon; Phobos; Poseidon; Sisyphus; Zeus.

ARIADNE

The daughter of King Minos of Crete and his wife Pasiphae, Ariadne played a crucial role in the slaying of the Minotaur by the Athenian hero Theseus. However, despite promising to marry her, Theseus later abandoned Ariadne on the island of Naxos.

Theseus arrived in Crete as one of the 14 young people sent every year from Athens, as reparation for the murder of a Cretan prince. They were all sacrificed to the Minotaur. This monstrous creature, half bull and half man, was the result of Pasiphae's unnatural coupling with the white bull of Poseidon. He was kept hidden in a palace of winding corridors and hidden rooms, the Labyrinth, built by the inventor and architect Daedalus. None of the young sacrificial victims had managed to kill the Minotaur or escape the Labyrinth.

Right: This carving on a fragment of a sarcophagus depicts Ariadne as a Cretan goddess of fertility. She is shown with Bacchus, the Greek god of wine and abundance, who fell in love with her.

Ariadne's plan

Ariadne caught sight of Theseus on his arrival in Crete and immediately fell in love with him. She promised to supply him with a way to escape from the Labyrinth if he agreed to marry her and take her back to Athens with him. Theseus agreed and Ariadne gave him a ball of twine (or, in some versions, golden thread) that Daedalus had previously given to her. By tying one end of the thread to the doorway at the entrance to the maze and then unraveling the ball as he went, Theseus was able to retrace his steps once he had slain the Minotaur.

When he emerged, Ariadne guided Theseus and the other surviving Athenians to the harbor, where they boarded his ship and fled toward Athens. At this point, the various versions of the myth diverge. In the most widespread version, the Athenian ship arrived at the island of Naxos and Ariadne fell asleep on the shore. Theseus embarked with his companions and abandoned her there. Ariadne awoke to find herself alone and deserted by her lover, for whom she had sacrificed family and homeland. However, Dionysus (Bacchus), the god of wine, had fallen in love with her and descended from heaven to carry her away to be his bride.

Variations in the legend

Another version of the myth says that Dionysus himself ordered Theseus to leave Ariadne, since the god had chosen her as his bride. Other variations tell that Ariadne was so distraught on waking and finding herself abandoned that she hanged herself. In yet another version of the myth, Theseus and the pregnant Ariadne were driven by a storm to Cyprus, where she died in childbirth.

Historical context and links

The story of Ariadne and Theseus illustrates the process whereby Athens freed itself from Crete, which, until about 1200 BCE, was a the leading power in the Mediterranean world. The Athenian Theseus puts an end to Cretan demands for reparations and gains a princess as his bride.

Ariadne herself, whose name means "most pure" or "most pleasing," was at one time worshiped as a fertility goddess in Crete and the eastern Mediterranean. Her union with Dionysus, the god of not only wine but also dance, excess, and abundance, seems to be a link between earlier Eastern and later Greek divinities of renewal and growth. A circular fertility dance led by Theseus is described in Callimachus's *Hymn to Delos,* written in the third century BCE, and Ariadne herself may well have led such a dance in Crete, on a labyrinthine-patterned floor constructed for this purpose by Daedalus.

The image of the solitary and inconsolable Ariadne was a popular theme in the visual art and poetry of antiquity, and she has remained a symbol of loss and abandonment in Western art. The Renaissance Italian artists Titian and Guido Reni both painted her, as did the French artist Jean-Baptiste Regnault at the start of the 19th century. In the early 20th century, Ariadne was the subject of an opera, *Ariadne on Naxos*, by German composer Richard Strauss. More recently, because of Ariadne's part in overcoming the horrors of the Labyrinth, her name has been used by a variety of projects related to information retrieval on the World Wide Web.

PETER CONNOR

Bibliography

Bulfinch, Thomas. *Bulfinch's Mythology.* New York: Modern Library, 1998.

Graves, Robert. *The Greek Myths*. New York: Penguin USA, 1993.

SEE ALSO: Bacchus; Crete; Daedalus; Dionysus; Minos; Pasiphae; Poseidon; Theseus.

Above: *A romantic vision of Ariadne imploring Theseus to marry her, painted by Jean-Baptiste Regnault (1754–1829). Theseus holds the ball of yarn aloft, like a trophy, before entering the Minotaur's Labyrinth.*

ARTEMIS

The Greek goddess Artemis (known to the Romans as Diana) was the daughter of Zeus (the ruler of the gods) and Leto, and the twin sister of Apollo. She was primarily the goddess of hunting. Wilderness, mountains, forests, and uncultivated lands were sacred to her, as were the young, and unmarried women.

Below: This painting by Italian artist Giovanni Battista Pittoni (1687–1767) shows Artemis surrounded by her attendant nymphs after Actaeon has been torn to pieces by his dogs.

Artemis was usually depicted as a young woman of marriageable age, dressed as a hunter, wearing a short tunic and sandals, with a quiver of arrows on her back, and carrying a bow. In literature she was often described as being accompanied by nymphs, with whom she danced and hunted in the mountains, far from the cities of mortals. She was thought of as an aloof goddess, bloodthirsty and quick to anger, whom it was dangerous to annoy or even to approach too closely.

Artemis was worshiped from very early times. Her name may appear on tablets from Bronze Age Greece (second millennium BCE), on which was written a script called Linear B that has only recently been fully deciphered. There is also evidence that her origins lay farther east than Greece. Her name is found among the gods of the Lydians of Anatolia (part of modern Turkey), who worshiped her as

"Artimus," and the Lycians of southwest Asia Minor (modern Turkey), who called her Ertemis. She was often shown in art accompanied by lions, which were also associated with cultures east of Greece, particularly, with the great goddess Kybele (or Anahita). The poet Homer, who wrote the *Iliad* and the *Odyssey* around 850 BCE, called Artemis the "mistress of animals," a title given to various West Asian goddesses, including the Assyrian Ishtar.

Powers at birth

Artemis was usually said to have been born to the goddess Leto on the island of Delos. According to Apollodorus, who collected and wrote down many Greek myths in the second century BCE, Artemis was midwife at the birth of her twin brother Apollo immediately after her own birth. Callimachus, a Greek poet of the third century BCE, says that the pregnancy and birth of Artemis gave Leto no pain, unlike the birth of Apollo. Whether because of her own painless birth or her help as a midwife, Greek women worshiped Artemis as a goddess of childbirth.

In Callimachus's "Hymn to Artemis," the goddess asked her father, Zeus, to allow her never to marry, to carry a bow and arrows, and to wear a short tunic that would allow her to hunt. She also asked for 60 young nymphs, around nine years of age, to serve as her companions, and another dozen, of marriageable age, to serve as her handmaids and keep her hunting dogs and clothes in order. Both of these age groups were important in the worship of Artemis in classical Greece.

Chased by gods and mortals

Artemis, like Athena, was a virgin goddess. Unlike Athena, however, Artemis found herself the constant object of male attention. She was depicted as an attractive, healthy girl, and therefore greatly sought after by men, who invariably died when they pursued her. Artemis shot and killed the giant Orion, a great hunter, for example. Some sources, such as Callimachus, say that Orion wanted to marry her. Other accounts say that she attacked him because he tried to rape her.

According to the Roman poet Ovid (43 BCE–17 CE) in his poem *Metamorphoses*, Actaeon was another hunter who died through the actions of Artemis. He stumbled upon her bathing in a stream with her nymphs and inadvertently saw her naked. To punish him, Artemis turned him into a stag and then set his dogs on him. They chased him and then ripped him to pieces, egged on by Actaeon's own friends, since he was unable to speak to tell them who he was.

The chorus of Artemis

Groups of young women dancing and singing in a chorus were a common feature of festivals in classical Greece. Such groups aroused keen male interest, since women lived largely segregated lives, and public festivals were one of the few opportunities young men had to inspect their

Right: *The Greek goddess Artemis was taken up by the Romans and renamed Diana. This Roman statue shows her with her hunting dogs, reaching for an arrow.*

Above: A woolen wall hanging embroidered on linen shows Actaeon and Artemis. The tapestry was made over 1,500 years ago.

future wives. Artemis's companions, the nymphs, were a reflection of this social reality in that they were described as persistently subject to male attentions, which were usually more successful than those received by the goddess herself. Thus Helen, who would cause the Trojan War, was said to have been kidnapped by Theseus from the chorus of Artemis. When the goddess Aphrodite disguised herself as a mortal in order to seduce the mortal Anchises, she told him that she had been dancing in the chorus of Artemis when the god Hermes had carried her off.

Often the attendant maiden's story had a tragic ending. Britomartis, a favorite companion of Artemis, threw herself off a cliff into fishermen's nets to escape a rape attempt by King Minos of Crete. She was turned into a sea goddess. In another story Zeus fell in love with Artemis's attendant Callisto. According to Ovid, Zeus disguised himself as Artemis in order to get close enough to Callisto to rape her. When Callisto's pregnancy was discovered, Zeus's enraged wife, Hera, turned Callisto into a bear. Apollodorus says that Artemis then shot her down as a wild beast, and the baby in her womb was rescued by the god Hermes. Ovid says that, after giving birth to Zeus's son, Callisto lived as a bear for years, until her son, Arcas, who had been raised by humans, met her in the forest, was terrified by her, and was about to kill her. Zeus saved him from the crime of killing his mother by turning them both into constellations, Big Bear and Little Bear (Ursa Major and Ursa Minor).

Artemis's favorites

From time to time Artemis made a favorite of a mortal, usually a young woman in her train. Callisto was one; Britomartis, Procris, Anticleia (the mother of Odysseus), and Atalanta were others. Eventually they were all forced to leave Artemis's band of maidens because they were married, raped, or, in the case of Britomartis, committed suicide to avoid rape.

One man, Hippolytus, was also a favorite of Artemis. He hunted with her and was permitted to hear her voice, although he was never allowed to see her. His story also ends tragically. Out of devotion to Artemis, Hippolytus refused to marry or have anything to do with mortal women. Aphrodite, the goddess of love, was angry at his neglect of her, so she set in motion a train of events that led to his death. Artemis mourned Hippolytus but could do nothing to protect him, because, as she explained, the gods never opposed each other directly over mortals; all she could do was promise to kill Aphrodite's next favorite, whoever he might be. The fullest account of this story is in the tragedy *Hippolytus*, by Euripides (c. 484–406 BCE).

Sacrifice to Artemis

Several Greek myths link Artemis with human sacrifice. The story of the sacrifice of Iphigeneia is the best known. It illustrates Artemis's touchy pride and fierce temper. Iphigeneia was the eldest daughter of Agamemnon, the leader of the Greek forces at Troy. While he was waiting for his soldiers to gather at the harbor at Aulis, Agamemnon shot a deer and boasted that not even Artemis could have made a better shot. Artemis took offense and sent an opposing wind that held the boats in harbor. She demanded as a price for a favorable wind the sacrifice of Agamemnon's daughter Iphigeneia, and he complied. Euripides' play *Iphigeneia at Aulis* tells how at the last moment Iphigeneia was miraculously replaced on the altar by a doe. According to Euripides, Artemis transported Iphigeneia to barbarian Tauris, on the Black Sea, where she became a priestess of Artemis at a temple that practiced human sacrifice.

The Greeks believed that the Taurians sacrificed humans to Artemis, and the inhabitants of Patrae told the second-century Greek writer and traveler Pausanias that at one time they had sacrificed a youth and a maiden every year

Artemis and Childbirth

Childbirth in the ancient world was much more dangerous than it is today. Artemis was the goddess of women's diseases, especially those associated with childbirth, and women approaching childbirth would pray to Artemis not to kill them during the birth, but assist them to have an easy and successful labor. If an Athenian woman died in childbirth, her friends or family would dedicate to Artemis clothing the dead woman had woven herself but never worn, at the temple at Brauron. It may seem odd that Artemis, the virgin goddess, would have also been the goddess of childbirth, but women at the threshold between maidenhood and marriage were sacred to her, and childbirth, as one of the main markers dividing virgins from wives, thus fell under her sphere of influence.

Below: *Worship of Artemis continued for thousands of years. This temple to her in Jordan survived until the second century CE.*

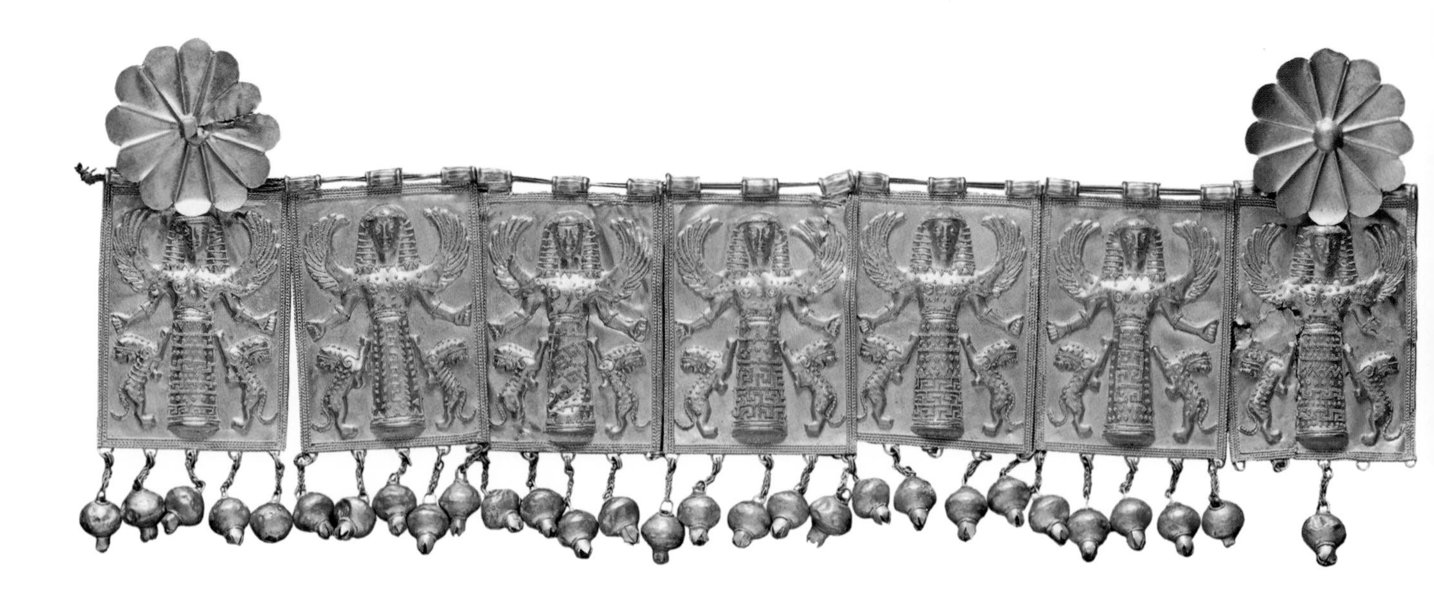

Above: Seven decorative gold plaques, worn across the chest with rosettes at the shoulders, show Artemis with lions. The item was found on the island of Rhodes and dates from around 700 BCE.

to Artemis, but they had stopped the practice around the time of the Trojan War, about 1,300 years before. In fact, all of the stories about Artemis and human sacrifice are derived from preexistent Bronze Age myths. There is no archaeological evidence that the Greeks ever made human sacrifices to Artemis. Instead, game animals—such as deer, boars, gazelles, and bear and wolf cubs—were commonly sacrificed to her, as well as goats. The inhabitants of Patrae in classical times held an annual festival in which game animals were burned alive to the goddess.

Artemis the nurse and protector

In her role as a goddess of childbirth, children and fertility came under Artemis's influence. Diodorus Siculus, a Roman–Greek historian of the first century BCE, tells us that Artemis was called Kourotrophos, or "child-rearer," because of her importance in the nursing and healing of the young. Groups of Athenian girls, at about the age of seven, were dedicated to the worship of Artemis in her temple at Brauron, near Athens, in a ceremony that involved games and races, at which the girls dedicated their childhood toys to the goddess.

Artemis was also protective of young animals. In one version of the sacrifice of Iphigeneia, Artemis demanded her sacrifice because she was angry at Agamemnon, who had been promised victory at Troy only if he slaughtered a pregnant hare. This anger would be expected in a hunting goddess, since no good hunter kills a pregnant animal.

If a woman was said to have been "killed by the arrows of Artemis," as Andromeda says of her mother in Homer's *Iliad*, it meant that she had died of disease. Artemis's influence in matters of fertility, her quick temper, and her power over diseases afflicting women are all shown in the story of Niobe. According to Homer, Niobe bore 12 children, while other sources say that she gave birth to up to 20. She boasted that she had done better than Leto, who had borne only Apollo and Artemis. To punish Niobe, Apollo set out to kill all of her sons, and Artemis to kill all of her daughters. Only one daughter and one son survived, after praying to Leto. Niobe turned to stone in grief.

Artemis in the arts

The tragic stories of the humans who associated with Artemis have inspired many artists. Titian (c. 1489–1576) painted the death of Actaeon, Diana (Artemis) and Actaeon, and Diana and Callisto; Rembrandt (1606–1669) depicted Diana bathing with her nymphs. The composers Charpentier, Cavalli, and Rameau wrote operas based on the myths of Actaeon, Orion, and Hippolytus. The American playwright Eugene O'Neill (1888–1953) adapted the story of Hippolytus in *Desire Under the Elms* (1924).

LAUREL BOWMAN

Bibliography

Euripides, and Paul Roche, trans. *10 Plays*. New York: Signet Classic, 1998.

Ovid, and A. D. Melville, trans. *Metamorphoses*. New York: Oxford University Press, 1998.

SEE ALSO: Actaeon; Agamemnon; Apollo; Atalanta; Britomartis; Callisto; Diana; Hippolytus; Iphigeneia; Leto; Niobe; Zeus.

ASCLEPIUS

Asclepius was the Greek god of healing and had sanctuaries throughout the Hellenistic world. People who were sick and did not want to go to a local doctor could go to one of the cool and pleasant places sacred to the god and seek a cure for their illnesses.

According to legend, Asclepius was the son of the god Apollo and a mortal woman, Coronis. However, his mother did not remain faithful to her divine partner. When a crow spied Coronis with a mortal lover, he flew to Apollo and reported what he had seen. Apollo became angry and asked his sister Artemis to kill Coronis. Coronis, who was still pregnant, died, but Apollo did not want his son to perish. He snatched the baby from Coronis's burning body and gave him to the wise centaur Cheiron to raise. It is said that Cheiron taught Asclepius the arts of medicine. In time Asclepius joined his father at Epidaurus in central Greece.

Although this is the most famous story of Asclepius's birth, other versions report that Coronis abandoned her newborn baby in shame on the mountain at Epidaurus. Goats nursed the child and a herd dog guarded him. When a local shepherd discovered the baby, lightning flashed about the child's head, and the shepherd left the infant to be raised by the goats and dog, under the protection of Apollo.

Apollo had many responsibilities, so Asclepius soon took charge of health and healing. However, as time went on, he became almost too clever at his work.

Asclepius cast out

One day Asclepius brought a dead hero back to life, allowing him to live longer than his fated destiny. Zeus, angry at this bold deed, blasted Asclepius down to the underworld. However, the world needed the god of healing, so Zeus restored the demigod to the upper world, where he stayed.

Using a walking stick with a serpent coiled around it and accompanied by a sacred dog, Asclepius traveled throughout Greece, curing the patients who came to the groves and medicinal springs where his sanctuaries had been established.

Asclepius was often assisted in his healing arts by three of his five daughters. The eldest, Hygieia, was best known; from her name comes our word *hygiene*. His other daughters were Iaso, whose

Left: Asclepius leans on his staff, around which a snake is twisted —this is now the symbol of the American Medical Association.

Above: A relief carved in the fifth century BCE shows Asclepius healing a patient, helped by his daughter Hygieia, right, while others wait for treatment.

name comes from a Greek verb meaning "to heal," and Panacea, whose name became the word *panacea*, which means "cure-all."

The sanctuaries of Asclepius

The most famous real-life sanctuary of Asclepius was at Epidaurus near the eastern coast of the Peloponnese (southern Greece). In the sacred area, entered by an elaborate gateway, were a temple to the god, the dormitory (*abaton*) where the patients slept, houses for priests and temple attendants, a large dining hall, and a hotel. There was also a mysterious round building known as a *tholos*. This beautifully decorated building had a circular maze in its basement. It is believed that the sacred snakes of the god were kept there until they were released to visit patients.

At Epidaurus and the god's other holy places, the patients were cured in a notable way. After bathing, singing hymns, and watching a dramatic story of the god's actions, they went to the *abaton* to sleep. It was believed that either the god or his snake visited the patients in their dreams, either curing their illness at once or telling them what to do to become healthy again.

At Epidaurus there was also a grand theater, where hymns and pageants for the god were sung and performed. Even today this theater, the best preserved in Greece, is used every summer for performances of ancient Greek tragedies and comedies. Asclepius also had large sanctuaries at Rome, Kos, Pergamum, and Athens. The sanctuary at Rome was established on Isola Tiberina, an island in the Tiber River, in 293 BCE after a plague attacked the city. To this day there are archaeological remains of a healing sanctuary on the island; a modern hospital stands above them.

Kos was the island where Hippocrates, the Father of Medicine, had his medical school, but Asclepius was also worshiped there. The connection between Hippocrates and Asclepius can still be recognized today. Every doctor must learn the Hippocratic Oath, and every U.S. doctor can be a member of the American Medical Association (AMA), whose symbol is a staff with a serpent coiled around it—the walking staff of Asclepius and his sacred snake.

Because of his healing powers and the legends of his life, Asclepius was one of the Greek gods who was worshiped long into the Christian era. His followers saw similarities between the stories of his birth and powers and those of Jesus Christ and could see no reason to change their beliefs. Finally, Christian churches were built to healing saints on the sites of the ancient temples to Asclepius; thus the old god was buried beneath the new religion.

KARELISA HARTIGAN

Bibliography

Graves, Robert. *The Greek Myths*. New York: Penguin USA, 1993.

Howatson, M. C., and Ian Chilvers. *Concise Oxford Companion to Classical Literature*. New York: Oxford University Press, 1993.

SEE ALSO: Apollo; Zeus.

ASTARTE

Astarte was a Phoenician fertility goddess and the wife and sister of Baal, the chief Phoenician deity. She was also the wife of El, the creator god of the ancient city of Ugarit. Although scholars know that she was an important deity, her many names and her similarity to many West Asian goddesses lend considerable confusion to her identity.

Above: This stone carving of Astarte, dating from the sixth century BCE, depicts her wearing a headdress, with hair flowing down her neck.

Astarte was undoubtedly an important deity, and she seems to have been the personification of the planet Venus. In ancient times the planets were regarded as bright stars. Venus was often regarded as two different stars: one that appeared in the morning, and another that appeared in the evening. The morning star was often given a male name, the evening star the name of a woman. The Phoenicians identified the evening star with Astarte.

A goddess of many names

Astarte was one of only a few goddesses mentioned in the Old Testament, where she was called Astoret or Ashtoroth. She was also worshiped by that name in the ancient cities of Phoenicia (modern Lebanon and Syria) in the first millennium BCE, but was so popular that she had many other names in different areas and at different times. For example, the Babylonians of the second millennium BCE called her Ashratu, which meant "Mistress of Abundance and Fertility." Not only did she have many names, but in each country or city Astarte might have a different family tree. Her name was known and she was worshiped outside Phoenicia all the way from southern Arabia to Egypt. In southern Arabia, she may have been connected with a cult of the sun.

She was also worshiped as the patron goddess of the city of Tyre, on the eastern Mediterranean coast, in the first millennium BCE, and the Greeks who settled along the coast of western Asia identified her with Aphrodite. In Egypt, she was at the height of her popularity between 1300 and 1000 BCE. There Astarte merged with other Asiatic goddesses. She sometimes appeared as a war goddess, sometimes as a fertility goddess, and sometimes as

Qadashu, a goddess of life and health. One of the oldest references to her comes from the city of Ugarit, modern Ras Shamra on the Syrian coast, in the mid-second millennium BCE In the legends from that city, there were three goddesses named Lady Asherah of the Sea, Astart-in-the-name-of-Baal, and Anat. Modern scholars are divided about which of these names refers to Astarte.

Lady Asherah of the Sea

To some scholars Lady Asherah of the Sea is another version of Astarte. That would make her the wife of El, the creator god of Ugarit, and mother of all the gods or wet nurse of the gods. Despite the maternal titles, however, she was not equally fond of all her children. Ugaritic legends say that she lived separately from El, in her own palace by the sea. This is not necessarily a sign that the goddess did not get along with her husband. The special palace was a sign of her importance and authority in the court of the gods. In spite of her authority, however, there were few mentions of her in the myths of that city.

However, there were stories of Baal, the fertility god, that were found in the archive of Ugarit. The scribes of Ugarit, like many other ancient West Asian peoples, wrote on baked clay tablets in cuneiform script (with characters formed from wedge-shaped impressions). These clay tablets usually survived because they were hardened by fire, but the various versions of the story of Baal have many gaps. The story that has been reconstructed seems to show that Lady Asherah of the Sea was the only one of the gods who could intervene on behalf of Baal. He had been asking the supreme god

Above: This gold pendant depicting the goddess is one of the earliest artifacts associated with Astarte. It was fashioned in Syria in the 14th century BCE.

Right: Astarte was the patron of Tyre, on the coast of Phoenicia. She was hated by the Hebrews, and Josiah (c. 640–609 BCE) destroyed all temples to her.

El for a palace, because he was the only god without a home. While Asherah was performing a ritual outside her seaside residence (or doing her laundry, modern scholars are not sure which), Baal and his consort Anat asked Asherah for her help.

Because she appeared frightened of this violent couple, some modern scholars have suggested that she had been plotting against Baal and that this would have been made clear in the lost sections of the text. However, without the missing pieces of the story, no one can say if she did in fact conspire against the storm god. The text that does survive states that Asherah was persuaded to saddle a donkey in order to ride to her husband. After discussion she managed to persuade El that Baal should have as magnificent a home as the other gods. Later, when Baal quarreled with a god

Syncretism

In the books of the Bible in which Astarte is mentioned, she is sometimes called Ashtoroth, which really means "the Astartes." Certainly the myths, which would have been familiar to most people in Biblical times, seem to speak of several goddesses performing the same actions, so this may be what is meant by *Astartes*. It might also be that the author of the books of the Bible in which the goddess is mentioned thought of each local version of her as a separate deity. Over time, however, the many goddesses of individual cities and myths merged, their names and personalities becoming interchangeable, a process called syncretism. The results of this blending, which happened over centuries, was evident even thousands of years ago as the cultures surrounding the Mediterranean in Europe, western Asia, and North Africa were changed and influenced by invasion, trade, and population migrations. The Astarte who was the end result of this process was an embodiment of the planet Venus and of the qualities of fertility and feminine sexuality.

Above: Three views of the goddess of fertility. Images of Astarte are sometimes described in the Bible as groves, a reference to the places where she was worshiped.

called Yam and was killed, one of Asherah's children was to be chosen to replace him on the throne. According to the story, Asherah had several sons. Her favorite was Ashtar, a male divinity who personified the morning star (Venus). Asherah suggested that he could be the next storm god, but he proved inept in the role.

Other scholars believe that the Ugaritic goddess "Astart-in-the-name-of-Baal" might be Astarte. In that case, she would be acting as Baal's champion, fighting for him. This role is also performed in some versions by Anat, a goddess known from Egyptian legends. Anat was similar to the Greek Athena: she never married or had children, and she dressed and acted like a male—in one text Anat seems to have had facial hair. Anat threatened her father, El, when he refused to grant Baal's wishes. Elsewhere in the legends of Baal, she was described as wading in blood. The similarity between Anat's actions and those of Astart-in-the-name-of-Baal has led some scholars to say that they are one and the same.

Possible depictions of Astarte

Because few of the ancient representations of goddesses of Canaan or Phoenicia were labeled, knowing what Astarte was supposed to have looked like is difficult. Since the Biblical version of her name may mean "horned," Astarte may be one of the goddesses represented wearing various types of horned crowns. Some of these headdresses consist of cowlike horns and a disk, similar to those of the great Egyptian goddess Hathor. Like images of Hathor, many of the pictures of the goddess show her with her hair parted in the middle and with two curls hanging over her shoulders. One ivory relief carving shows a winged goddess with horns and a disk suckling two standing figures.

As a goddess of fertility, Astarte may have been the divinity shown nude and represented facing the viewer in two-dimensional art such as relief carvings. She might also be shown holding plants, symbolizing her power over the fertility of growing things. Since Astarte was associated with horses, images of a nude female on the back of a horse may also be her. Astarte is described in the epic poem *Paradise Lost* by the British poet John Milton (1608–1674). Milton analyzes the causes of the Fall of Man, and describes the false gods worshiped by the people of Canaan:

> "With these in troop
> Came Astoreth, whom the Phoenicians call'd
> Astarte, Queen of Heav'n, with crescent Horns;
> To whose bright Image nightly by the Moon
> Sidonian Virgins paid their Vows and Songs."

LYN GREEN

Bibliography

Roaf, Michael. *The Cultural Atlas of Mesopotamia and the Ancient Near East.* New York: Checkmark Books, 1990.

SEE ALSO: Baal; Canaan and Phoenicia; Fertility; Stars.

ATALANTA

In Greek mythology Atalanta was beautiful, strong, and the fastest runner of the mortals. She traveled with Jason and his Argonauts on the search for the Golden Fleece, but she is most famous for her adventures after the quest, including the Calydonian boar hunt, the race with Hippomenes, and for misbehaving in a temple of Zeus.

***Right:** Even in marble, Atalanta looks strong and athletic. This statue dates from the fourth or third century BCE.*

Atalanta's mythical origins are not certain: some tales say that she was the daughter of Schoeneus of Boeotia, others that Iasus of Arcadia was her father; and there are hints that her mother may have been an attendant of Artemis, the Greek goddess of the hunt. Whoever her parents were, legend tells of a dramatic childhood. When Atalanta was newly born, her father was so disappointed in not having a son that he abandoned the infant in the forest, where she was rescued and nurtured by a bear. Some time later hunters found the bear suckling the baby, and they took her to raise as their own. Atalanta grew up to be a fine archer and hunter.

Some scholars argue that for the ancient Greeks the myth of Atalanta highlights prejudice in favoring sons over daughters. At the same time Atalanta's fictional story fits into a pattern seen in the lives of many mythical heroes. For example, Paris, Oedipus, and Orestes were all abandoned or rejected when young, but legends tell how they survived, succeeded, and fulfilled the fears or desires that prompted their parents to abandon them. Atalanta not only became as strong and successful as any son her father could have wished for, she went on to deny her femininity by rejecting the idea of marriage. She was also the prototype for other female warriors, such as Camilla, who is featured in Book 11 of the *Aeneid* by the Roman poet Virgil (70–19 BCE).

In terms of the chronology of Greek mythology, Atalanta belonged to the generation before the Trojan War, and she participated in the two major heroic expeditions of her fictional time: the quest for the Golden Fleece with the Argonauts and the Calydonian boar hunt. In one account, however, Jason, the Greek hero who led the Argonauts, dissuaded Atalanta from joining the quest because he feared that a woman's presence would spark conflict among his men.

The boar hunt

After the Golden Fleece adventure, Atalanta played a more important role in the Calydonian boar hunt. When King Oeneus of Calydon offended Artemis by failing to offer her a sacrifice, the goddess sent a terrible boar to ravage Calydon. Oeneus's son Meleager, who had been one of the youngest Argonauts, summoned all his erstwhile companions, including Atalanta, to help him destroy the boar. During the hunt Atalanta took first blood from the boar by shooting an arrow into its head. Although the wound did not kill the beast, it made it easy for the others to finish off the boar, with Meleager delivering the final deathblow. Meleager awarded the prize of the boar's skin to Atalanta. This angered the rest of the hunters, especially Meleager's maternal uncles, Plexippus and Toxeus, because they did not believe such an honor should go to a woman. In the ensuing dispute Meleager killed both his uncles. This proved Meleager's undoing.

Meleager had been cursed at his birth by the Fates—three women who controlled destiny. The Fates had

Left: This painting by Flemish artist Peter Paul Rubens (1577–1640) depicts the moment when Meleager awarded the boar's head to Atalanta.

appeared to Meleager's mother, Althaea, and predicted that her son would live only as long as the log that was burning in the fireplace remained intact. Althaea had immediately pulled the log from the fireplace and guarded it to protect Meleager. When Althaea heard that her son had slain her own brothers, she angrily threw the fateful log into the fire, causing Meleager to die.

The race

According to legend, Atalanta's success in the Calydonian boar hunt prompted a reconciliation with her father, Schoeneus or Iasus. Like all fathers of ancient Greece, real or fictional, Schoeneus or Iasus had a social responsibility to find his daughter a husband. Yet Atalanta spurned wedlock, possibly because she had been warned against it by an oracle, or fortune-teller. The gods rarely tolerated women who refused to marry, so to appease the gods and her father, she agreed to marry on one condition. The man she married would first have to beat her in a footrace, but the losers would be killed.

Atalanta, who was the fastest mortal on earth, always won the races, even when she gave her opponents a head start. The death toll of failed suitors mounted. Finally Hippomenes (or Melanion in some versions), who was in love with the beautiful Atalanta, took up the challenge.

Meanwhile, Aphrodite, the goddess of love, had grown tired of Atalanta's deadly game, and she gave Hippomenes three golden apples from the garden of the Hesperides, maidens who guarded a magical tree. During the race Hippomenes distracted Atalanta by rolling each apple just far enough ahead of her that she would stop to pick it up. By doing this three times, Atalanta slowed enough for Hippomenes to win the race.

Atalanta kept to her word and married Hippomenes. The couple grew to love each other and all seemed well. Then one day Aphrodite, who had grown enraged because Hippomenes had failed to thank her properly for the golden apples, cast a spell on the newlyweds, causing them to make love in the temple of Zeus. The king of the gods saw the couple in his temple and as a punishment turned Hippomenes into a lion and Atalanta into a lioness. Another version has it that the couple were caught in the temple of Cybele (Rhea), mother of the gods. She then turned the lovers into lions and hitched them to her chariot to serve her forever.

Atalanta in art

The stories about Atalanta have inspired several artistic masterpieces. Peter Paul Rubens (1577–1640) painted *Meleager and Atalanta* around 1635: it depicts Meleager offering the trophy of the boar's head to Atalanta. Rubens completed *The Hunt of Meleager and Atalanta* some years earlier. This artwork shows Atalanta at the moment just after she shot the arrow into the boar, while Meleager stabs the beast with a spear. Today the painting is housed in the Kunsthistorisches Museum in Vienna, Austria.

Guido Reni (1575–1642) painted Atalanta and Hippomenes around 1612. In Reni's painting the two runners are almost nude. Hippomenes, who is ahead of Atalanta, has just thrown another golden apple and Atalanta stoops to pick it up. Since the late 19th century the painting has hung in Madrid's Prado Museum.

KATHRYN CHEW

Bibliography

Bulfinch, Thomas. *Bulfinch's Mythology.* New York: Modern Library, 1998.

Howatson, M. C., and Ian Chilvers. *Concise Oxford Companion to Classical Literature.* New York: Oxford University Press, 1993.

SEE ALSO: Animals; Aphrodite; Artemis; Fates; Jason; Virginity; Zeus.

ATE

Ate was a mischief-making goddess who, the ancient Greeks believed, drove mortal men to folly and self-destruction. She was thrown out of Olympus, home of the gods, by her father, Zeus, who was angry at her rebellious behavior.

Ate was the goddess of discord and delusion. She was expelled from the home of the gods because she clouded Zeus's mind when he made Eurystheus a king instead of Heracles. There is a hill in Phrygia named for Ate, and it was believed to have been the spot where she landed when Zeus threw her out of Olympus.

Ate inspired infatuation, bringing mortal men under the power of women and clouding their judgment. During the Trojan War, for example, Agamemnon, king of Mycenae, took the mistress of his finest warrior, Achilles, as his own. Later he blamed Ate for his actions.

Origin of Ate

Ate's origin goes back some five thousand years, to when patriarchal tribes invaded the lands of the goddess-worshiping peoples of the Mediterranean. They substituted their sky gods for the mother goddess who, it was believed, had embraced both life and death. After the belief in sky gods took over in Europe, however, many maternal deities lost their creative qualities and came to represent death. The goddess Ate was one of them. The Greeks feared the goddesses they had displaced, such as Ate, and perhaps thought that ancient earth deities like her wanted to avenge their lost power.

Occasionally in Greek drama and mythology, Ate had a role of enforcing moral conduct. She was a variant of the Furies, who hounded men to madness if they broke sacred family laws; and like the Furies, she avenged crimes against her Olympian relatives.

Parallels to Ate also exist in other cultures. In Norse mythology, for example, Brynhild, the Valkyrie, was a daughter of Odin and visited warriors about to die on the battlefield. Her disobedience to her father was one of the reasons for Ragnarok, the ruin of the Norse gods.

BARBARA GARDNER

Left: This painting by German artist Johann Heinrich Tischbein (1722–1789) depicts the moment Achilles nearly draws his sword on Agamemnon, only to be stopped by the cloudy figure of the goddess Athena. According to the myth, the goddess Ate prompted Agamemnon to start the dispute.

Bibliography

Bulfinch, Thomas. *Bulfinch's Mythology.* New York: Modern Library, 1998.

Homer, and Robert Fagles, trans. *The Iliad.* New York: Penguin USA, 2003.

SEE ALSO: Achilles; Agamemnon; Earth Mother; Furies; Nemesis; Odin; Valkyries; Zeus.

ATHENA

Athena, the favorite daughter of Zeus, was the Greek goddess of wisdom, crafts, and war. Some say she created the bridle, showed men how to make and use a plow, and invented the trumpet. She was the guiding deity of Athens and gave the olive tree as a gift to the city. The owl was her favorite bird, and she is often shown with a coiled snake at her feet. Her cult came to Rome from Etruria, where she was called Minerva.

According to most sources of Greek mythology, Athena was born from the head of Zeus, ruler of the gods, and she was always his favorite daughter. One myth says that Zeus had been told that his first wife, Metis, goddess of intelligence, was destined to have a child who would eventually overthrow him, just as he had overthrown his own father, Cronus. To prevent this, Zeus swallowed Metis. (Other versions of Athena's birth claim that she had no mother and that she, not Metis, was the goddess of wisdom.) Then one day Zeus had an extremely painful headache and asked the Olympians to help cure it. Some versions of the story report that Prometheus, a Titan, stepped forward to strike the royal head with an ax; others say it was Hephaestus, god of metalwork and fire. When Zeus's head was split, Athena sprang forth wearing full battle armor and helmet, holding her spear in one hand and shield in the other (see box, opposite). In that account and others of the goddess of war, Athena was described as appearing with bright eyes flashing and her armor

***Right:** Athena's helmeted head is all that remains of this mid-second century CE Greek statue.*

gleaming. Another source says that when she made her first appearance in front of the Olympians, all nature responded to her, the earth shook and the seas rose in huge waves, until the sun god, Helios, stopped his chariot and made the world stand still to honor the new goddess.

Athena was often called Pallas Athena (see box, page 172). Some sources claim that Pallas was the name of a favorite friend of Athena's—in one version her lover—whom she killed accidentally, and so out of guilt and grief she adopted Pallas's name as part of her own. Another name the Greeks added to hers was Tritogeneia. According to the Greek poet Hesiod, who lived around 800 BCE, *Tritogeneia* meant "she who was born on the banks of the river Triton," but the relevance of the name is unclear.

The defeat of Typhon

In one early Greek myth Athena showed her courage above all other gods when she single-handedly defended Mount Olympus, the home of the gods, when it was under threat from Typhon. Typhon was the largest, strongest, and most frightening monster on earth, and when he tried to climb Mount Olympus, all the other gods fled in terror. Only Athena remained, battling the monster while at the same time goading her father, Zeus, into action. Eventually Zeus regained his courage and returned to the battleground, striking the monster with his thunderbolts. Then Athena (or Zeus, depending on the version) threw Mount Etna on top of Typhon, crushing the monster underneath. It was believed that the volcanic rumblings of Etna were the moans of Typhon (or Cronus, according to some versions.)

The contest with Arachne

Zeus's favorite daughter shared many of the interests and abilities of her father. Yet very much unlike her lascivious father, Athena was not linked romantically to any other Olympian deity, nor did she have sexual relations with mortal men. She always remained a virgin goddess.

Athena, although goddess of war, also cared for the concerns of women, especially their important skill of weaving. It was believed that Athena would carefully guide a woman's hand as she wove the clothes for her family. Yet Athena was also vain about her own weaving and did not tolerate being challenged.

One young girl, Arachne, made the mistake of thinking that she was better at the loom than Athena, so she challenged the goddess to a weaving contest. Athena easily won the competition and to teach the arrogant girl a lesson, she changed Arachne into a spider, who would spend the rest of her days weaving webs. From this myth comes the modern classification name for spiders, *arachnids*.

Athena's Battle Dress

During times of peace Athena usually wore a peplos, the same type of garment the other Olympian goddesses wore. When a war or battle began, however, she put on her armor, which included a helmet, and picked up her spear or lance and a shield made from the tough skin of the giant Pallas. It was the same battle dress she had worn when she emerged from her father's skull.

In addition to the regular battle dress, she also wore Zeus's aegis, a goatskin cloak or breastplate with gold tassels. According to one version, the aegis would conjure storms and thunder when shook. Some descriptions of the aegis have it that in the center was embroidered the head of a Gorgon, a female monster with snakes for hair. Others claim that it was Athena's shield, not the aegis, that bore the image of a Gorgon's head. She also had another weapon in her arsenal. Because Athena was Zeus's favorite daughter, he allowed only her to summon his mighty thunderbolts during battle. However, she usually relied on her own strategic cunning and finesse to win her fights.

Left: Pallas Athena in her full battle dress is the subject of this 17th-century painting. The work has been attributed to Rembrandt.

Origins of Pallas Athena

As with most Olympian gods, Athena originated in cultures outside the Greek mainland. Early archaeological evidence shows that Athena's prototypes were mostly bird and snake goddesses. One of the earliest prototypes of the Greek Athena was a Minoan, or Cretan, snake goddess who was the patron of many female domestic skills, such as weaving, pottery making, and cooking. It is also thought that the Minoan priestesses of Athena were expert snake handlers. Athena's close association with snakes was maintained in early Athens, where an Athena figurine found in a tomb had snakes for arms, leading some scholars to assert that at one time Athena was considered a snake goddess of the underworld. Neith was an early snake goddess from Egypt, who was closely associated with vultures, as was Athena, and oversaw domestic skills. A third influence was the Canaanite deity Anat, again a snake goddess. The ancient Libyans of north Africa also had a goddess of snakes, death, and sun. The Libyan Pallas was a cattle deity and a war goddess. She was said to have been born from Lake Tritonis, near one of the areas believed to have been the home of the Amazons. Her worship was brought to the Greek islands by the Libyans as they emigrated across the Mediterranean sea. The Hellenes brought her to Athens around 800 BCE, where she merged with Athena.

Athena in battle

When a war began, Athena's attention focused on the soldiers, especially those who fought most heroically or were the leaders of the armies. Several heroes gained Athena's particular affection and assistance. For example, when Orestes, son of Agamemnon (king of Mycenae and leader of the Greek forces in the Trojan War), was on trial for killing his mother, Clytemnestra, who had murdered Agamemnon, Athena voted that Orestes be pardoned. The goddess argued that the father is the most important parent, so Orestes' crime was not as bad as that of Clytemnestra.

In Homer's *Odyssey* (c. 850 BCE), Athena most admired the hero Odysseus. Although the goddess could not spare him from the dangers Poseidon put in his way, she did make sure Odysseus survived them. When at last she revealed to him who she was and what she had done for him, she also told him why she cared for him. "You are so careful, your mind is so clever, Odysseus, and so I have always looked after you." Then the goddess helped her hero return safely to his palace in Ithaca.

Aiding Heracles

A third hero Athena assisted was Heracles. As a son of Zeus and the mortal Alcmene, Heracles had some divine blood (ichor) in his veins and superhuman strength. Nevertheless, he still needed the help of Athena, because Hera, wife of

Left: A Roman statue of Athena wearing her battle helmet and aegis, with the Gorgon's face on her left shoulder. Her spear is missing.

Below: Dating from around 1430, this painted plate depicts a contemporary version of Paris judging the beauty contest between the goddesses Hera, Athena, and Aphrodite.

Zeus and the queen of the gods, was jealous of Alcmene and made sure that Zeus's son by her suffered. Hera arranged for Heracles to act as a servant to King Eurystheus of Tiryns and Mycenae. Eurystheus forced Heracles to complete 12 Labors. Athena could not stop Hera's plans for Heracles any more than she had been able to overcome Poseidon's obstacles against Odysseus. However, she made sure Heracles successfully completed all of Eurystheus's tasks. In reference to the story, many vase paintings of Heracles show Athena by his side. In the myth of Heracles' mortal death and ascension to Mount Olympus, it was Athena who served him wine.

Judgment of Paris and the Trojan War

The goddess Athena played a central role in an important Greek legend, the story of the Trojan War. The story began with an episode of jealousy, vanity, and desire known as the Judgment of Paris. Zeus chose Paris, a prince of Troy who was considered the handsomest man in the world, to judge a beauty contest between Athena, Hera, and Aphrodite, goddess of love. Another version of the episode did not include Zeus but had Eris, goddess of strife, throwing the Apple of Discord to the goddesses. A message on the apple said that it was to be awarded to the fairest of all the goddesses. Together the three goddesses called on Paris to decide who most deserved the apple. While Paris was deliberating, Athena promised Paris wisdom and military skill if he chose her as the most beautiful, Hera offered the rule of a mighty kingdom, and Aphrodite told him that the most beautiful mortal woman in the world would be his if he voted for her. For Paris, Aphrodite's offer was the most tempting, so he chose the goddess of love as the winner. From that moment on both Hera and Athena vowed to harm Paris and Troy.

Although Aphrodite kept her word and introduced Paris to Helen, the most beautiful woman, one large problem remained. Helen was married to Menelaus, king of Sparta. The only way Paris would be able to have Helen was to steal her from Sparta. Paris's abduction of Helen sparked the Trojan War, an epic conflict between Greece and Troy that lasted 10 years. The war split the Olympians between those gods that supported the Trojans, such as Ares and Aphrodite, and those that intervened on behalf of the Greeks, including Hera and Athena. A few gods remained neutral or acted arbitrarily, most notably Apollo and Zeus.

Athena stepped in on the side of the Greeks at several crucial times. One example was when Achilles, the Greeks' best warrior, was about to draw his sword on his ally Agamemnon, Greek king of Mycenae and brother of Menelaus. Achilles was angry because the Greek leader had insulted him. Just as Achilles was about to draw his sword, Athena stood invisible behind him and caught hold of his hair. In the *Iliad* she says, "I have come to stop your anger. Do not take your sword in your hand. You may abuse him with words but do not fight him." Achilles obeys. He goes on to slay many Trojans, most famously their champion Hector, the brother of Paris.

Above: Athena featured in vase paintings, such as on this amphora made in the sixth century BCE. The Gorgon is depicted on Athena's shield.

Athena and the fall of Troy

Athena played another important role in the fall of Troy. She helped the Greek carpenter Epeios build the Trojan Horse. Odysseus is said to have had the idea of the large wooden horse, but it was Epeios, aided by Athena, who actually constructed it. The wooden horse was left as a gift to the Trojans, who, thinking the Greeks had given up the war and left, wheeled it into the city. That night the few Greek soldiers who were hiding in the horse's belly emerged from the structure and opened the city's gates. The Greek army quickly returned, captured Troy, and killed nearly all the men, including Paris, who died from a poisoned arrow.

While Troy was under siege and the Greeks were pillaging, Ajax of Locris (also known as Ajax the Lesser; not to be confused with Ajax of Salamis, a Greek hero of the war) pursued the cursed soothsayer Cassandra, Priam's daughter, into Athena's temple. The frightened girl clung to the deity's image, but Ajax pulled her away and raped her. Athena determined he would suffer for his sexual violation of her temple. Ajax managed to survive the stormy seas she sent to hinder his trip home, and standing on a cliff he boasted that he had overcome the storm and conquered both Athena and Poseidon. At once the sea god sent an earthquake that split the cliff from the land, plunging Ajax into the waves and drowning him.

Patron of Athens and Bearer of Olive Oil

When Athens wanted a guiding deity, two Olympians, Poseidon and Athena, vied for the position. Poseidon struck the earth with his trident and a horse sprang forth (some versions have him bringing forth a saltwater spring). Athena touched the ground with her spear and an olive tree grew. The Athenians decided that the hilly countryside had no fields for horses and that the olive tree was the better gift. It was from that moment, according to legend, that Athena became the patron of Athens; in return the Athenians adopted the owl, Athena's symbol, as their own.

Athena's gift of olive oil became one of the most important products in the ancient world and helped to make Athens wealthy. Women used it in their face and body creams and perfumes, for burning in lamps, and in cooking. It was used by men in their athletic competitions. They would put oil on their bodies before their contests, then at the end scrape off the oil and sand with a special curved bronze tool called a strigil. Large jars, known as amphoras, of olive oil were given as prizes in athletic contests held annually in Athens. Olive oil also formed part of the healing lotions Greek warriors used after battle.

Right: *Athenians stamped an owl on their coins in honor of their patron, Athena. This Athenian coin was made in the sixth century BCE.*

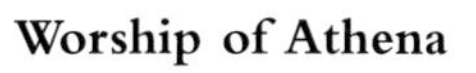

Worship of Athena

Athena was worshiped in temples all over the Greek world, but her most famous sanctuary was the Parthenon, named for Athena's cult, Parthenos, meaning "Athena the Virgin." The Parthenon was built atop the Acropolis in Athens. Most Greek cities had an acropolis, which was a high fortified compound usually in the center of a city, inside which religious rituals took place and where, it was believed, the gods came to dwell. It was also where the citizens retreated during a siege. The acropolis in Athens is the best known, mainly because of the Parthenon. An earlier temple to Athena on the Acropolis had been burned during the Persian invasion of Greece in 480 BCE, and the Parthenon replaced that temple.

The political force behind the building of the Parthenon was Pericles (c. 495–429 BCE), the architects were Ictinus and Callicrates, and the artistic superviser was the sculptor Phidias (or Pheidias; c. 490–430 BCE). Together these men were responsible for the construction of one of the world's most important and influential buildings. The Parthenon, built entirely of marble, was designed in the Doric style of architecture, the simplest of the classical orders, or styles of building, and constructed between 447 and 432 BCE. The outside of the Parthenon has a colonnade of 8 columns along the front and back and 17 along each side. On the west, or back, pediment (the triangular section shaped by the roof above the columns) were sculptures of Athena and Poseidon offering their gifts to the Athenians (see box, above): the olive tree grows before Athena, a horse prances by Poseidon. On the east pediment the sculpture showed Athena being born from the head of her father, Zeus, while all the gods and goddesses watch the event. Phidias designed these and the other sculptures on the temple, which are now in the British Museum, London, England.

Around the wall of the temple itself, inside the colonnade, ran a long series of marble figures. They represented the citizens of Athens at the Panathenaea, a festival in honor of Athena held in the city every spring. Also shown were the gods and goddesses whom the citizens believed came to their ceremonies.

Statues of Athena

Inside the Parthenon stood a giant statue of Athena also designed by Phidias. Covered in gold and ivory, the statue was 36 feet (11 m) tall and showed the goddess wearing a peplos, the aegis, and an elaborate helmet; she held a spear in one hand and a statuette of the goddess of victory, Nike, in the other. Beside her was her shield with the Gorgon's head at its center, an owl, and the sacred snake. The citizens of Athens made sacrifices to their goddess on the altar in front of the temple, but they went into the Parthenon to worship before the giant statue of Athena. Another statue of the goddess stood in the center of the hill. Made of bronze, the deity's spear was so large and gleamed so brightly in the sun that, according to legend, it could be seen by sailors far out at sea.

A second, smaller temple was built at the western edge of the Acropolis. This one was also dedicated to Athena, but this time for her role as goddess of Athenian victory. The Nike temple is in the Ionic style (slightly more ornate than Doric) and has columns only on its front and back. On the protective wall setting of the temple was carved an image of the goddess untying her sandals, a symbolic message to the Athenians that she would always protect their city.

At the north side of the Acropolis stands a third temple. It is called the Erechtheum and was dedicated to the deities Athena and Poseidon, and to two mythic kings of Athens, Cecrops and Erechtheus. The interior held the tombs of these kings and a lamp lit with special olive oil. The east porch was dedicated to Athena, and inside stood the oldest statue of the goddess on the Acropolis. This simple wooden statue was believed to have fallen from the sky to Athens.

On the south side of the Erechtheum is another small porch also sacred to Athena. There the columns are in the form of six maidens bearing baskets on their heads. These statues, called caryatids, represent the women who carried gifts for the goddess in an annual but secret ceremony. Today the caryatids are housed in a museum for protection, and

replicas of the maidens support the porch roof. A porch on the north was dedicated to the god Poseidon. The Athenians believed that it protected the mark made by his trident when he created the horse as his offering to them. In an enclosure on the west flourished the olive tree given by Athena as her gift to the people of Athens.

KARELISA HARTIGAN

Right: *This 19th-century color illustration is an artist's impression of the giant statue of Athena by the Greek sculptor Phidias. The original statue was gold and ivory and stood in the center of the Parthenon. In her left hand Athena holds a statue of Nike, the deity of victory.*

Below: *The Parthenon, a temple to Athena, was built in Athens in the mid-fifth century BCE and is considered one of the world's great structures.*

Bibliography

Bulfinch, Thomas. *Bulfinch's Mythology.* New York: Modern Library, 1998.

Homer, and Robert Fagles, trans. *The Iliad.* New York: Penguin USA, 2003.

SEE ALSO: Aphrodite; Arachne; Ares; Cassandra; Crete; Diomedes; Gorgons; Helen; Hera; Heracles; Minerva; Nike; Odysseus; Orestes; Paris; Poseidon; Typhon; Virginity; Zeus.

ATLAS

Atlas was a Titan who was forced by the Greek god Zeus to bear the weight of the heavens on his shoulders. The image of him struggling under his great burden is still familiar today, mainly because of his widespread depiction in art.

The Titans included the children of Uranus and Gaia, the primordial god and goddess, as well as some of their grandchildren. Atlas's father was Iapetus, one of the six sons of Uranus and Gaia, and his mother was Clymene. His brothers included Prometheus and Epimetheus. They were respectively the fathers of Deucalion and Pyrrha, the only survivors of the great flood sent by Zeus to exterminate the human race. Atlas was thus uncle to the parents of the whole race of mortals.

The children of Atlas

Although his brother Prometheus was a more prominent benefactor of the human race, bringing fire to the world, Atlas also had close links to humankind. The ancient Greeks believed that about one third of the great dynasties of Greece were descended from a group of seven of his daughters, including the ruling families of Troy, Sparta, Mycenae, and Thebes. These daughters were collectively known as the Pleiades. Through one of these daughters, Maia, Atlas was the grandfather of the god Hermes, and several others of the Pleiades either married or bore children by the gods Zeus, Poseidon, and Ares.

Another batch of Atlas's daughters, the Hyades, were nurses to the god Dionysus. Later sources say that Atlas was also the father of the Hesperides, a group of nymphs who lived on an island at the end of the world. In the *Odyssey*, meanwhile, Homer (c. ninth–eighth century BCE) writes that Atlas was the father of Calypso, the nymph with whom Odysseus stayed on his way back to Ithaca.

Long before mortals were created, the Titans, under the leadership of Cronus, defeated their father Uranus and took over the universe. The Titans were in turn deposed by Cronus's son Zeus and Zeus's siblings, known as the Olympians for their home on Mount Olympus. The war that the Olympians waged against the Titans was known as the Titanomachy. The struggle between the two rival powers lasted for 10 years, and after he had led his forces to victory, Zeus cast the Titans down to Tartarus, the deepest part of the underworld.

For Atlas, however, Zeus reserved a special fate. Because of Atlas's great size and strength, Zeus made the Titan stand in the far west, beyond the Mediterranean Sea, holding the heavens on his broad shoulders. Atlas was destined to bear the weight of the heavens for all eternity. Because of his fate, his name is sometimes interpreted as meaning "the Bearer" or "the Endurer."

Atlas and Heracles

The best-known myth involving Atlas also featured the Greek hero Heracles. To make amends for an earlier crime, Heracles was forced to serve Eurystheus, the king of Tiryns and Mycenae, for 12 years. Eurystheus ordered Heracles to carry out the famous 12 Labors of Heracles.

One of Heracles' Labors was to bring King Eurystheus the golden apples of the Garden of the Hesperides. The tree bearing the golden apples had been a gift from Gaia to Hera, queen of the gods, when she married Zeus. The tree was guarded by a dragon. On his way to the Garden of the Hesperides, Heracles came across Atlas's brother Prometheus. After Heracles shot the eagle that Zeus had sent to torment him, Prometheus advised Heracles that Atlas, the father of the Hesperides, was best suited to retrieve the apples.

Heracles eventually found the Titan, who agreed to help him. However, someone would have to hold up the heavens while Atlas was away. That burden fell to Heracles, who was aided by the goddess Athena. Atlas retrieved the apples. He enjoyed the freedom from having to carry his great load so much that he told Heracles he would gladly take the golden apples to Eurystheus himself. However, Heracles easily tricked Atlas into returning to his position

Right: *The Italian artist Giovanni Francesco Barbieri, also called Il Guercino (1591–1666), painted this version of Atlas holding the heavens. The heavens are depicted in the form of a globe.*

by asking him to help for a moment while he adjusted the pillow he was using as a pad for his shoulders. When Atlas took the weight of the heavens from him, Heracles stepped away to leave the Titan to bear the weight for all eternity.

The Atlas Mountains

Today Atlas is also identified with a large mountain range that runs through present-day Morocco, Algeria, and Tunisia in north Africa. In ancient times, the Atlas Mountains formed a famous, almost impenetrable barrier between the Mediterranean coastal region and the Sahara Desert inland. As early as the fifth century BCE, the Greek historian Herodotus referred to the Atlas Mountains as the "pillars of heaven." The mountain range begins in the west of Morocco, near the Atlantic coast. To the ancient Greeks, this would have been the very end of the world, where Atlas would have been made to stand by Zeus.

Another legend tells a different version of how Atlas was turned into stone, however. According to the Roman poet Ovid (43 BCE–17 CE), the hero Perseus stopped in the land of the Hesperides after successfully decapitating the Gorgon Medusa, whose glance turned people to stone. He asked the region's king, Atlas, for hospitality. However, an ancient prophecy had said that a son of Zeus was destined to steal the golden apples, so Atlas turned Perseus away. In response to this insult, Perseus took Medusa's head from his wallet. Even dead, the Gorgon turned King Atlas into a stone mountain.

Links with Atlantis

Atlas was also associated with the fabled land of Atlantis. The Greek philosopher Plato (c. 428–c. 348 BCE) recounted in two of his later works, *Timaeus* and *Critias*, that 9,000 years before there had existed a huge island paradise in the far west, way beyond the Pillars of Heracles (the modern Strait of Gibraltar). The island continent was called Atlantis and, according to Plato, was rich in natural resources. On it lived a people ruled by a dynasty of kings descended from the god Poseidon. According to Plato, the civilization there became very advanced and built an empire that extended from the far west into the Mediterranean, as far as today's Italy and Egypt. Plato's tale also described how the first inhabitants of Atlantis were an

__Below:__ The snow-capped peaks of the Atlas Mountains in northern Africa. The mountains have long been associated with the Titan.

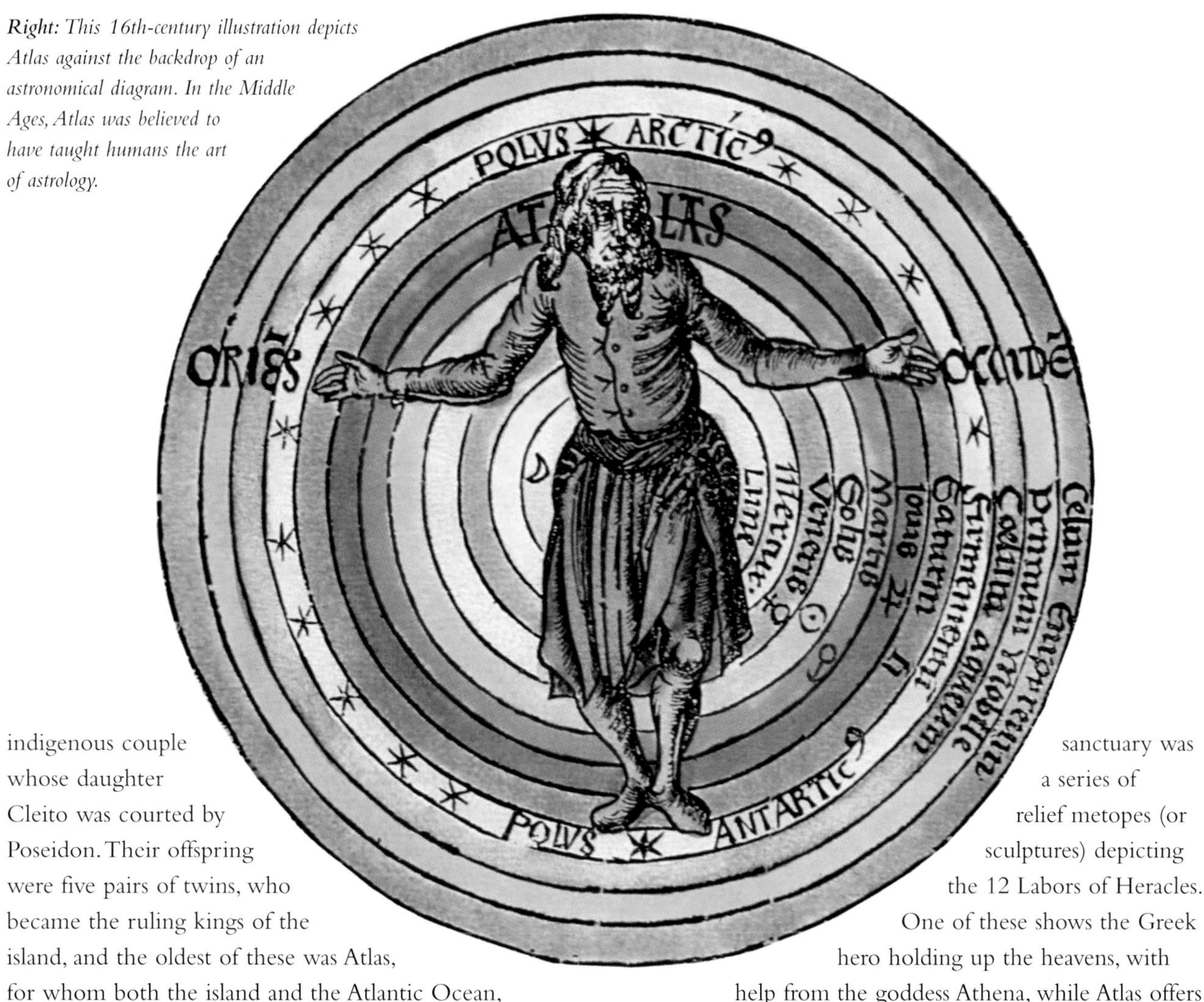

***Right:** This 16th-century illustration depicts Atlas against the backdrop of an astronomical diagram. In the Middle Ages, Atlas was believed to have taught humans the art of astrology.*

indigenous couple whose daughter Cleito was courted by Poseidon. Their offspring were five pairs of twins, who became the ruling kings of the island, and the oldest of these was Atlas, for whom both the island and the Atlantic Ocean, were named. (Today, most scholars believe that the Atlantis myth was based on the volcanic eruption of the Mediterranean island of Thera around 1600 BCE.)

Atlas depicted in art

Over the centuries Atlas has been a popular subject for painters and sculptors. Among several significant works that depict him is *Atlas* by the 17th-century Italian artist Giovanni Francesco Barbieri. The painting shows a powerful and muscular Atlas bending under the weight of the great globe that he is holding up. Atlas is depicted in a similar pose in the Farnese Atlas, which is housed at the National Archaeological Museum in Naples. This is probably the most famous statue of Atlas and dates from the second century CE. It is possibly a Roman copy of a Greek statue. The statue features the earliest known depiction of a celestial globe, a map of the heavens in globe form.

The myth of Heracles and Atlas is depicted in several famous works of art from ancient Greece. One example was found in the Temple of Zeus in Olympia, the site of the ancient Olympic Games. In the middle of the temple's sanctuary was a series of relief metopes (or sculptures) depicting the 12 Labors of Heracles. One of these shows the Greek hero holding up the heavens, with help from the goddess Athena, while Atlas offers him the apples of the Hesperides.

From Atlas's role as bearer of the heavens on his shoulders come several modern uses of the word *atlas*. Using the word *atlas* to denote a collection of maps comes from the practice of using a picture of the Farnese Atlas bearing the world (the orb of heaven that he carries being mistaken for Earth) as a frontispiece to collections of maps. The practice was made popular by the famous 16th-century geographer Mercator. In anatomy the atlas is the top cervical vertebra, which supports the skull, while in architecture an atlas is a male figure used as a column to support a roof or balcony.

ANTHONY BULLOCH

Bibliography

Bulfinch, Thomas. *Bulfinch's Mythology*. New York: Modern Library, 1998.

Ovid, and A. D. Melville, trans. *Metamorphoses*. New York: Oxford University Press, 1998.

SEE ALSO: Athena; Calypso; Crete; Cronus; Flood Myths; Gaia; Gorgons; Heracles; Hesperides; Odysseus; Poseidon; Prometheus; Titans; Uranus; Zeus.

ATREUS

Atreus and his extended family featured heavily in Greek drama and mythology. The family was collectively known as the House of Atreus, and its story revolves around themes of jealousy, revenge, sex, and power. The focus of the family battles and intrigue tended to be the throne of Mycenae, which both Atreus and his brother Thyestes occupied at different times.

***Below:** The cliffs of north Zákinthos, an island west of the Peloponnese Peninsula. The Peloponnese was named for Pelops and was the battleground for the power struggle between Atreus and his brother.*

Like a modern soap opera, the rivalry between Atreus and his brother Thyestes lasted many years and included plots of intrigue, murder, incest, and adultery. It also blighted the lives of the two kings' children and grandchildren. Atreus and Thyestes were sons of Pelops and Hippodameia (also spelled Hippodamia), and it was with them that the dramatic story began. Pelops, for whom the Peloponnese (or Peloponnesus) was named, was the son of Tantalus, king of Sipylus, and Hippodameia was the daughter of Oenomaus, king of Pisa in Elis.

Before Pelops could marry Hippodameia he first had to face Oenomaus in a chariot race. If Oenomaus won the race, then Pelops would be killed but if Pelops won, then he could marry Hippodameia. To ensure victory Pelops bribed Oenomaus's charioteer, Myrtilus, to sabotage his master's chariot. Oenomaus was killed and Pelops won the right to marry Hippodameia. After the race, however, Myrtilus demanded his payment: Pelops had promised him a night

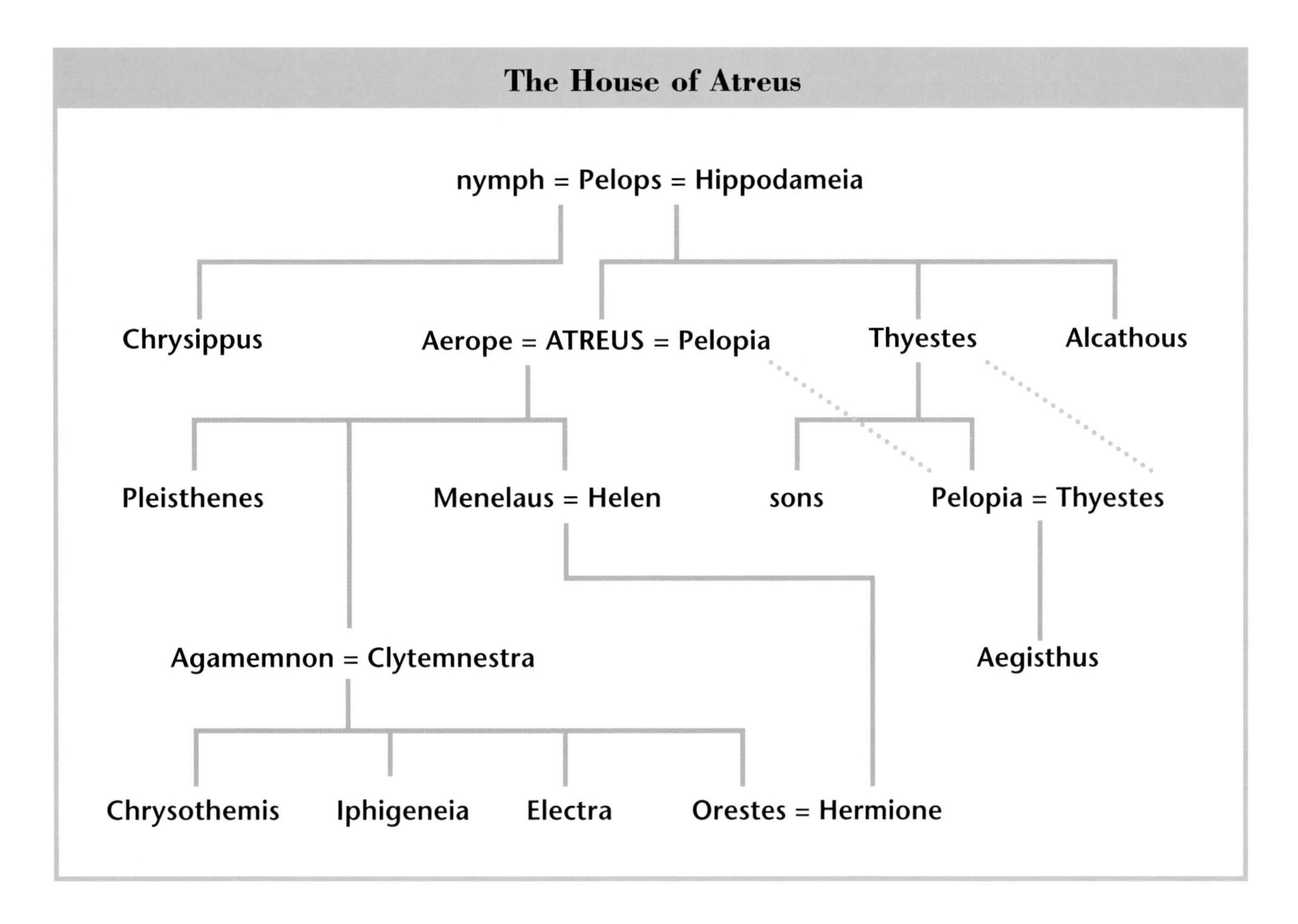

with Hippodameia. Instead Pelops killed Myrtilus, who, before he died, cursed Pelops and his children. According to some versions of the story of the House of Atreus, it was Myrtilus's curse that began the troubles for the family.

The throne of Mycenae

The House of Atreus was one of the major dynasties to feature in the plays and stories of the dramatists of ancient Greece. Traditionally the descendants of Pelops were associated with the settlement and political development of large areas of the northern and central Peloponnese Peninsula. Several of Atreus's brothers (not all of whom are shown in the family tree, above), for example, were believed to have ruled important cities in the eastern area of the Peloponnese, including Troezen, Sicyon, and Epidaurus. Atreus and Thyestes were closely linked to the Argolid, the eastern Peloponnesian Plain that includes the historical cities of Argos, Mycenae, Tiryns, and Nauplion. The sons of Pelops came to the Argolid after they were expelled by their father for murdering Chrysippus, Pelops's son by a nymph whom he had married before Hippodameia. As the oldest son, Chrysippus was heir to Pelops's kingdom. (In another version, Chrysippus committed suicide, after he was abducted and raped by another man, Laius.)

Atreus and Thyestes settled near Mycenae, which was ruled by Perseus's grandson Eurystheus. Eurystheus's father had married one of Pelops's daughters, so Eurystheus was the nephew of the two brothers. When Eurystheus died, an oracle prophesied that one of the two sons of Pelops would inherit the throne.

Atreus, who was the older brother, had the stronger claim to the Mycenaean throne, but Thyestes proposed that whoever possessed a certain golden lambskin should become king. The prized lamb had been given to Atreus as a cursed gift by either the god Hermes, father of Myrtilus, or by the goddess Artemis as a test to see if Atreus would willingly sacrifice it to her. Atreus, assuming the lambskin was still safely locked away, agreed. Unknown to Atreus, however, Thyestes had earlier seduced Atreus's wife, Aerope, and persuaded her to give him the golden lambskin. When Thyestes presented the prize, he became king. Atreus, realizing he had been tricked, convinced Zeus to help him win the throne. Zeus made the sun move backward in the sky. The Mycenaeans recognized this as a sign that identified Thyestes as a usurper.

Not satisfied with having become king, Atreus wanted revenge for Thyestes' seduction of Aerope. He threw a banquet in his brother's honor, and all seemed to have been

The Treasury of Atreus

Atreus's name was given to the most famous piece of architecture to survive from the Mycenaean civilization, the Treasury of Atreus. The structure was originally a tomb that would have included valuable grave goods, but it was plundered thousands of years ago. No one knows the name of the king who was buried there. Archaeologists believe that the tomb was built between 1300 and 1200 BCE. It was carved into a hillside and was made of rectangular blocks of stone stacked in 33 rows. It is an example of a *tholos*, or beehive tomb, so called because the shape of its dome resembles a beehive. Inside the tomb the rotunda is 44 feet (13.5 m) high and 48 feet (14.6 m) wide. The pathway leading up to the doorway of the tomb is 115 feet (35 m) long, flanked by high walls. The facade was originally richly decorated, and some of the reliefs survive in museums around the world, such as in Athens, Berlin, and London.

Below: *The Treasury of Atreus was the tomb of a Mycenaean ruler whose identity is unknown. The triangle above the doorway is typical of ancient Mycenaean architecture.*

forgiven. After the main course had been consumed, Atreus revealed the severed limbs and heads of Thyestes' sons cooked in a stew. Thyestes realized he had already eaten the flesh of his sons. Following the gruesome banquet, Atreus banished Thyestes from Mycenae. According to some versions of the legend, it was Thyestes, not Myrtilus, who then placed a curse on the House of Atreus.

Thyestes' revenge

While in exile, Thyestes learned from the Delphic oracle that to avenge himself he had to have a son by his own daughter, Pelopia. One night he disguised himself and slept with his daughter, who did not know his true identity. Another version of the story tells that Thyestes raped a priestess whom he spied bathing in Sicyon after she had conducted nocturnal rites to Athena. Unknown to him, the priestess was actually Pelopia, and he left without either father or daughter realizing the other's identity.

Meanwhile, Atreus had killed Aerope for her infidelity, but not before she had given birth to his sons Agamemnon and Menelaus. Soon afterward, on a visit to Sicyon, Atreus

fell in love with and married Pelopia, whom he assumed was a Sicyon princess, the daughter of King Thesprotus. Several months later Pelopia gave birth to a son, Aegisthus; unknown to Atreus, the infant was Thyestes' son, not his.

Years later Atreus sent Aegisthus on a mission to assassinate Thyestes, whom Atreus had captured and imprisoned in Mycenae. As Aegisthus approached, Thyestes recognized the sword the young man was carrying as his own. At the time of the rape, Pelopia had stolen Thyestes' sword from its scabbard and had later given it to Aegisthus. Instead of killing Thyestes, Aegisthus murdered Atreus and made his real father king of Mycenae.

In a different version of the story, another one of Atreus's sons was Pleisthenes, who was sometimes spoken of as the father of Agamemnon and Menelaus, making them actually the grandsons of Atreus. When Thyestes went into exile after his attempt to acquire the throne of Mycenae, he took Pleisthenes with him, pretending that he was his own son, not the son of Atreus, who was also ignorant of his paternity. Later Thyestes sent Pleisthenes back to Mycenae with instructions to kill Atreus, which induced Atreus to have Pleisthenes killed, thus unwittingly murdering his own son.

Agamemnon's death

When Agamemnon grew up, he overthrew Thyestes and became king of Mycenae. He then killed Tantalus, one of Thyestes' sons, and married Tantalus's widow Clytemnestra, the sister of Helen. Agamemnon and Clytemnestra had three daughters, Chrysothemis, Iphigeneia, and Electra, and a son, Orestes. Meanwhile Menelaus had become king of Sparta and had taken Helen as his wife.

Right: *This Greek amphora was made sometime between 340 and 330 BCE. The artwork illustrates the story of Atreus, including on the top row the murdered king on his throne.*

While Agamemnon and Menelaus were leading the Greek forces during the Trojan War, Aegisthus became Clytemnestra's lover. When, after 10 years, Agamemnon returned to Mycenae, the lovers murdered him. Later the lovers were killed by Orestes. After a long period of insanity, Orestes himself became king of Argos and Sparta.

Sources and dramatizations

Classical scholars believe that the major sources for the epic story of the brothers Atreus and Thyestes, the unfaithful Aerope, and the young Pelopia were two lost plays by Sophocles, a fifth-century-BCE Greek dramatist, and that the dramatic life of the rivalry between Atreus and Thyestes was a popular subject on the Athenian stage from the fifth century BCE onward. However, none of the plays that survive by the other major dramatists of ancient Greece —for instance, Aeschylus and Euripides—deals directly with either brother.

Yet some important surviving works do tell the story of the younger generation of the House of Atreus. The main examples are Aeschylus's *Agamemnon* and Euripides' *Electra* and *Orestes,* which are still performed by major theatrical companies. Also, a play called *Thyestes,* by Roman dramatist Seneca (c. 4 BCE–65 CE), describes the butchering of Thyestes' children.

ANTHONY BULLOCH

Bibliography

Aeschylus, and Robert Fagles, trans. *The Oresteia.* New York: Penguin USA, 1984.

Euripides, and Paul Roche, trans. *10 Plays.* New York: Signet Classic, 1998.

Harding, Anthony. *The Mycenaeans and Europe.* San Diego: Academic Press, 1997.

SEE ALSO: Agamemnon; Clytemnestra; Helen; Iphegeneia; Menelaus; Orestes; Pelops; Tantalus.

ATTIS

Attis was a Phrygian fertility god whose death and resurrection were commemorated every year by the Phrygians, and later the Romans, to celebrate the start of spring. In most mythologies there are tales of gods or goddesses who were worshiped in order to ensure good harvests every year, but in most cases they are characterized as female. Attis was depicted as a beautiful—and sometimes as an effeminate—male.

The story of Attis (also spelled Atys) was set in Phrygia (modern-day Anatolia, which forms part of central and western Turkey). It has many parallels with the tale of the Greek god Adonis, although there are several versions of the birth, loves, and death of Attis. One element is consistent: Attis came back to life.

Tales of birth and love

One account of the birth of Attis describes his mother as Nana, a water nymph. Nana, a virgin, placed on her breast a pomegranate from a tree that was created from the blood of the male sexual organs of Agdistis, a hermaphrodite. (Some versions suggest that an almond was used; according to other accounts, Nana ate the fruit.) There are also myths that describe Attis as the son of Cybele, the mother of the gods. Although it is not clear how he was conceived, no intercourse was involved. It is even possible that Cybele and Agdistis were one and the same character.

Whatever the circumstances of his birth and parentage, in every version of the story Attis grew into a pretty young man (he was sometimes described as effeminate) and became a shepherd. Because of his beauty Cybele grew obsessed with him. When the shepherd fell in love with a nymph, a curse was placed on him, which caused him to go insane and castrate himself. It is sometimes told that Cybele cast the spell to prevent Attis from ever loving anyone else.

One version gives Cybele a more active role. After she had cast her spell, Attis ran wildly through the woods, eventually falling into a drunken sleep. While he was asleep Cybele tied

Right: A marble bust of Attis shows him wearing a Phrygian cap. This soft, close-fitting felt headwear was later worn by freed slaves in Rome as a symbol of their liberty.

Right: This silver-and-gold plate shows Attis and Cybele riding in a procession, surrounded by dancers. It was made in Italy in the fourth century CE and was used to make offerings to the gods.

Attis's penis to her own foot. When he woke and tried to run, his penis was torn off and he soon died.

Violets sprang from Attis's blood, and the gods brought him back to life, never to age or decay. In some versions Attis was transformed into a pine tree, and pine trees played an important role in his worship. (In a few versions Attis, like the Greek god Adonis, was killed by a wild boar, but while violets sprang from Attis's blood, in Adonis's case it was buttercups.) The resurrection of Attis symbolized the start of spring.

Introduction to Rome

The Phrygian myth of Attis and Cybele was introduced to Roman society around 204 BCE, when Rome was under threat from the Carthaginian general Hannibal (247–183 BCE). To boost Roman morale the authorities took advantage of a prophesy claiming that bringing Cybele to Rome would eventually force the retreat of Hannibal. A Roman envoy was sent to Phrygia to retrieve an ancient black stone that was said to embody the mother of the gods. The stone was housed in the temple of Victory on Rome's Palatine Hill. Within a year Hannibal was forced to return to Carthage.

Over the following two to three centuries the importance of Attis as a fertility god spread throughout the Greek and Roman worlds, and Attis was invested with celestial and solar attributes, eventually becoming a symbol of immortality. At the same time a cult grew around the myth of Attis. The priests of the cult were known as the Galli, and they supposedly castrated themselves in a fit of orgiastic frenzy during a special initiation ritual—although it is possible that they merely drew blood. The tale of a young man who fell into such a frenzy of devotion and castrated himself is told in a poem by the Roman poet Catullus (c. 84–54 BCE).

The worship of Attis's sacred pine tree, with the god's effigy bound to its trunk, was incorporated into the established religion of Rome and celebrated as a festival that began on March 22 and lasted several days. On March 23 there was an extended period of mourning. On the following day, the spring equinox, the resurrection of Attis was commemorated during the festival of Hilaria (Joy). This was a time of carnival and masquerading. Two days later the whole festival came to a close with a solemn procession to the waters of the Almo stream.

There was also a more private celebration that included a sacramental meal and an initiation ritual held on the Vatican Hill (the site of St. Peter's Basilica) in which a bull was slaughtered over a grating, beneath which the initiates were bathed in the fresh blood. Similar rites were performed in Gaul (modern France) and in Germany.

CARL RUCK

Bibliography

Frazer, James George. *The Golden Bough*. New York: Simon and Schuster, 1996.

Wiseman, T. P. *Catullus and His World: A Reappraisal*. Cambridge: Cambridge University Press, 1985.

SEE ALSO: Adonis; Blood; Fertility; Ishtar; Mithraism; Rebirth.

ATUM

The ancient Egyptian god Atum was the creator of the world. In the earliest accounts, he was the first to emerge from primeval waters, taking the form of a hill. He was also worshiped, with Re (or Ra), as a sun god, but later the two deities were combined as Atum-Re. Atum represented the setting sun, Re the sun at its highest point in the sky.

Above: *Atum (left) wears the double crown, signifying the unification of the Upper and Lower Kingdoms. Here he leads Sesostris I (also known as Senusret I), ruler from 1917 to 1872 BCE. Sesostris is wearing the crown of Lower Egypt. Both figures carry an ankh, the symbol of life carried only by gods and kings.*

The ancient Egyptian civilization lasted for more than 3,000 years, so there are wide variations in its myths about the various gods and goddesses, their relative importance, and the names given to them. One thing that all the various religious texts have in common is the emphasis on the importance of the sun. To the priests and people of the city of Heliopolis (the Greek name for the Egyptian city of Iunu, which was close to modern-day Cairo), Atum was the sun. He was also the god of creation and symbolized the fertility of all living creatures.

Atum the creator

The cult of the sun was formalized in Heliopolis during the period referred to as the Old Kingdom, around 2650–2150 BCE. According to the local creation myth, in the beginning there was nothing but Nun, the primordial waters. Out of the waters, Atum was born. At first he appeared as a pyramid-shaped hill, known as Benben. This outcrop, which was at Heliopolis, was considered to be the first land to emerge from the primeval water, and the top of it was the first place to feel the light of the sun.

Atum then set about his task of creating other gods and goddesses. Since he had no goddess with whom to conceive a child, texts explain that he produced two gods from his own bodily fluids. They were Shu, the god of the air, and Tefnut, the goddess of the water.

The next two deities to be created were the goddess Nut (the sky) and the god Geb (the earth), who are often depicted in carvings and paintings as an arch, with Nut forming a rainbowlike arc over Geb. In order to bring balance to the universe, and to create order out of the chaos that had gone before, Atum is sometimes reported to have forced Nut into this arch shape, giving space for the air and everything else in the world between the earth and the sky. Geb and Nut created a further four gods: Osiris and his wife Isis, and Seth and his wife Nepthys.

These nine gods, headed by Atum, formed the Great Ennead of Heliopolis, which dates from the Third Dynasty (2650–2575 BCE). *Ennead* was a Greek word meaning "a group of nine." In Egypt, however, not all enneads consisted of nine gods. The Egyptian equivalent, *Pesdjet,* meant any group of gods.

Atum-Re and the sun cycle

Over the centuries Atum's status in Heliopolis as a sun god changed subtly. First he was replaced by an all-powerful sun god, Re (or Ra), and then he became merged with Re as Atum-Re (or Re-Atum). Atum was considered to be part of the daily cycle of the sun across the sky. The sun at dawn was Khepra, represented by a beetle perpetually rolling a ball of dung that symbolized the solar disk in its course. At noon it was Re, and at sunset it was Atum. This cycle perpetuated the original significance of Atum as god of death and resurrection, because the daily journey of the sun was seen as a symbol of the cycle of life, where every living creature is born (Khepra), grows up (Re), and then dies (Atum).

In his role as the setting sun, some texts describe Atum as having to fight the snake god Apophis every evening. Apophis was the symbol of chaos and lived in the waters beneath the earth, where the sun traveled at night.

Animal depictions

In some versions of the creation myth, Atum grew from a sacred serpent called Imy-uaf, translated as "Slithering One." His serpent nature is depicted in the uraeus, the cobra head set in the crown of the pharaohs, which represented constant awareness of Atum, since the cobra lifts its head up when it senses danger, just as Atum did during creation. The pharaohs of Egypt had a godlike status and were regarded as the sons of gods—often the sons of Re.

After his identification with Re, the sun god was also represented as the Mer-ur, better known by its Greek name Mnevis, a black or spotted bull with the uraeus on its forehead. He was also sometimes represented as a man with a bull's head crowned by a solar disk, feathers, and the uraeus between its horns. The creature was considered to be the *Ba* or "life force," the double of Re, and also the intermediary between gods and men.

This has parallels in the Greek Minotaur, whose parents were the Cretan king Minos and his wife Pasiphae. Because Minos did not sacrifice the bull Poseidon sent him, the god made Pasiphae fall in love with it. The result of this union was the Minotaur, a being that was half man, half bull. Just

Above: *Evenings along the Nile often take on a magical atmosphere, when the setting sun, associated with Atum, glows red on the horizon.*

The Sun Gods of Egypt

Atum, Re, and Atum-Re were not the only sun gods in Egyptian mythology. At Thebes (modern Luxor), the sun god had the name Amun (or Amen), and later became combined with Re as Amun-Re. Many of the pharaohs of Egypt adopted the name of the sun god as part of their title. Tutankhamen, who lived in the 14th century BCE, is the best-known example—his name meant "living image of Amun." Amun was worshiped at the temple of Karnak in Thebes.

Aten, another sun god, only had a short spell of rule in mythology. Aten was worshiped by a predecessor of Tutankhamen (possibly his father or uncle). Originally known as Amenhotep IV, he changed his name to Akhenaten ("He who is of service to Aten"). After being crowned at Karnak, Akhenaten felt that the power of the priests of Amun was becoming too great, so he decided that everyone should worship just a single god, Aten. Like the sun itself, Aten was all-powerful. Akhenaten built a new city dedicated to Aten, called Akhetaten ("Horizon of Aten"), and moved there with his queen, Nefertiti. He renamed his queen Neferneferuaten ("beautiful is the beauty of Aten"). Akhenaten ordered all the temples to Amun to be closed. He promoted the arts in his new city, and carvings show a much more relaxed style of portraiture, with the royal family worshiping a radiant sun god, depicted as a solar disk with rays reaching down to the earth, and hands at the end of each ray, ready to help the mortals on earth. After Akhenaten's 17-year reign, the cult of Amun was restored under Tutankhamen.

Above: *Atum (or Re), in his form as a cat, attacks Apophis, the serpent representing chaos. Behind Apophis is a sacred tree, known as the Ished tree. Although it is not known exactly which species this tree was, it is likely to have been from the same plant family as the bay tree.*

as Mer-ur was son of the cow goddess Ihet and was related to the cult of the sun, Pasiphae was the daughter of Helios, the Greek sun god.

Atum was also represented as a weasel or a mongoose, animals that hunt and kill snakes, which made the Egyptians believe they were immune to snake venom, just as Atum was immune to the attacks of Apophis. Elsewhere, Atum was variously depicted as an eel, a cat, a man with a ram's head, a small lizard, and a baboon armed with a bow and arrows.

Below: Atum-Re sometimes took the form of a bull known as Mnevis. In the mythology of Memphis, Ptah the creator also took this form and was known as Apis. The bull was a symbol of strength and masculinity.

The Benu bird

Atum was also associated with a bird known as the Benu, which is said to have flown over the waters of Nun before the original creation. The bird came to rest on a rock and its call was the first sound ever made. (The Greek equivalent of the Benu is the phoenix.) Although Egyptian writings describe the Benu as a type of wagtail, most representations show a beautiful heron that symbolizes the birth and rebirth of the sun. The Benu lived in its own mansion at Heliopolis, near Benben. According to the Greek writer Herodotus (c. 484–c. 425 BCE), the Benu resembled an eagle. The fantastic bird was supposed to live for five hundred years. At the end of its lifespan, it died in flames. Some people maintained that it burned itself on a pyre at the top of an obelisk (or on Benben). According to others, the Benu was sacrificed by the priests of Heliopolis. Since there was only ever one of the species, as soon as it died it was immediately born again by hatching from an egg that appeared in its own ashes.

Parallels and conflicts

Egyptian mythology has several other creation myths, based on other characters and described by priests from different religious centers. While the people of Thebes had Amun as the creator (see box opposite), in Memphis (Inbw-hedj), Ptah was the god of creation. Ptah was able to create gods and the earth by spitting or by simply saying the names of the forms he created. In order to make their religion appear superior to that of Heliopolis, the Memphis priests credited Ptah with the creation of Atum. Ptah was the original spirit and also took the form of eight elements of the creation story. The most powerful and versatile of these elements were Niu and Naunet. Niu was the spirit of primeval waters and the father of Atum; Naunet gave birth to Atum, and to a lotus that carried Atum ashore.

Yet another myth, from the city of Hermopolis (Khmun in ancient Egypt, halfway between Luxor and Cairo), describes the creation as starting from an Ogdoad (a group of eight gods) who lived in the primeval waters and created the first land, which took the form of a mound where the city stood. They then produced a cosmic egg, from which the sun god hatched. The sun god then went on to create the rest of the universe.

José Alfredo González Celdrán

Bibliography

Hobson, Christine. *The World of the Pharaohs.* New York: Thames and Hudson, 1990.

Redford, Donald B. *The Ancient Gods Speak: A Guide to Egyptian Religion.* New York: Oxford University Press, Inc., 2002

See also: Animals; Creation Myths; Egypt; Geb; Nut; Isis; Osiris; Re; Seth.

AUSTRALIA

Stories about mythological ancestors and other beings lie at the very heart of the traditional life and culture of the Aboriginal people, the earliest inhabitants of Australia. The myths set out the fundamental doctrines that were the basis of shared morality and law, and they gave an explanation for the existence of the cosmos, the land, waters, sky, stars, and the Aboriginals themselves.

The Aboriginal people of Australia came to the island more than 40,000 years ago. They developed a close relationship with their environment and an intricate belief system that linked the land, their day-to-day lives, and mythical ancestors. The land provided all their needs: the people lived by hunting, gathering wild foods, and fishing.

When the British colonization of Australia began in 1788, some 500,000 or more Aboriginal people inhabited the continent. Most Aboriginals now live in Australia's arid interior, but when the first colonists arrived, most inhabited the coasts and river valleys. In the deserts, the Aboriginal population was sparse—only about one person per 40 square miles (103 sq km)—and the people were very mobile. Along major waterways, such as the Murray River, or on the coast, people were more settled, and population densities were as high as one person per square mile in some regions.

In the desert, Aborigines lived in camps with an average number of 15 residents in each. Camps on the coast, where shellfish, fish, and turtles were readily available, were larger, typically with between 40 and 50 inhabitants. Coastal settlements broke up into smaller groups in some seasons and came together into larger groups of a hundred or more at others. Because food was plentiful, camps on the coast moved only a few times a year and not very far.

The members of an Aboriginal camp lived in separate family groups but cooperated in food production. Because communities were small, people often married someone from a distant camp to avoid inbreeding and to ensure that camps across a wide region were linked by ties of marriage and family. Aboriginal people spoke about 250 distinct languages and many more dialects. In some places the name of the local language, such as Arrernte or Warlpiri, gave its name to each group of several hundred people. Elsewhere people were known by the name of the area in which they lived, such as Krauatungalung, "people of the east," in Victoria. Aboriginal society was egalitarian: there were no national or tribal governments. Older people had the most authority, but individuals could gain influence and social status by being strong fighters, religious leaders, or healers.

At the beginning of the 21st century, Aboriginal people of full and mixed descent live in large coastal cities and in country towns, as well as on former reserves and missions. In these regions, in the southeast and southwest of the continent, traditional religions were largely destroyed during the 19th century. In more remote parts of Australia, Aboriginals live in small communities on their own lands. Ownership of these lands by Aboriginals was recognized by Land Rights laws passed in the 1970s. In these areas some people still practice traditional religions but incorporate elements of Christianity.

Aboriginal religions

Unable to identify gods and goddesses or worship, early settlers in Australia misunderstood Aboriginal religion. Some colonists thought the Aborigines had no religion. In time, complex systems of belief that varied from place to place were recognized. It is difficult to know how many religions there were, because one merged into another.

Below: *Uluru in central Australia, also called Ayers Rock, has great religious significance for the local Aboriginal people, who believe that the area around it was home to many ancestral beings.*

At the center of all Aboriginal religions is a belief in a creative era at the start of time. In English, this era is called the Dreaming or Dreamtime. In Dreaming, spirits wandered through a world that had no form. These spirits created all the elements of the physical landscape: the mountains and hills, rivers, lakes, and water holes, as well as the trees and bushes. On a larger scale, the spirits fashioned the sky, the sun and moon, and the stars. Aboriginal people believe that these spirit beings now inhabit organisms, such as trees, and places, such as lakes and rocks. The belief that organisms and places are inhabited by spirits is called animism.

The creator spirits made all the living creatures: the birds, mammals, insects, fish, and reptiles, as well as the Aborigines themselves. The creator spirits, and other beings who lived long ago, were like humans—they camped, hunted, made love, fought, and performed ceremonies, just like people do now. Many of these spirits were of extraordinary size, however, and all had great power.

Totemism

The area of land shaped by ancestral spirits is called a Dreaming Track. Each group has its own Dreaming Track, the place where the group was created and now belongs. Groups of Aboriginals are identified with species of animals, plants, birds, or celestial objects such as the sun or moon. For example, one Aboriginal group calls itself the Emu people and another the Shark people. Identification with animals or objects is called totemism.

According to Aboriginal beliefs, spirit beings with the identity of emus were the ancestors of the Emu people, and similar beings with the identity of crocodiles were the spirit

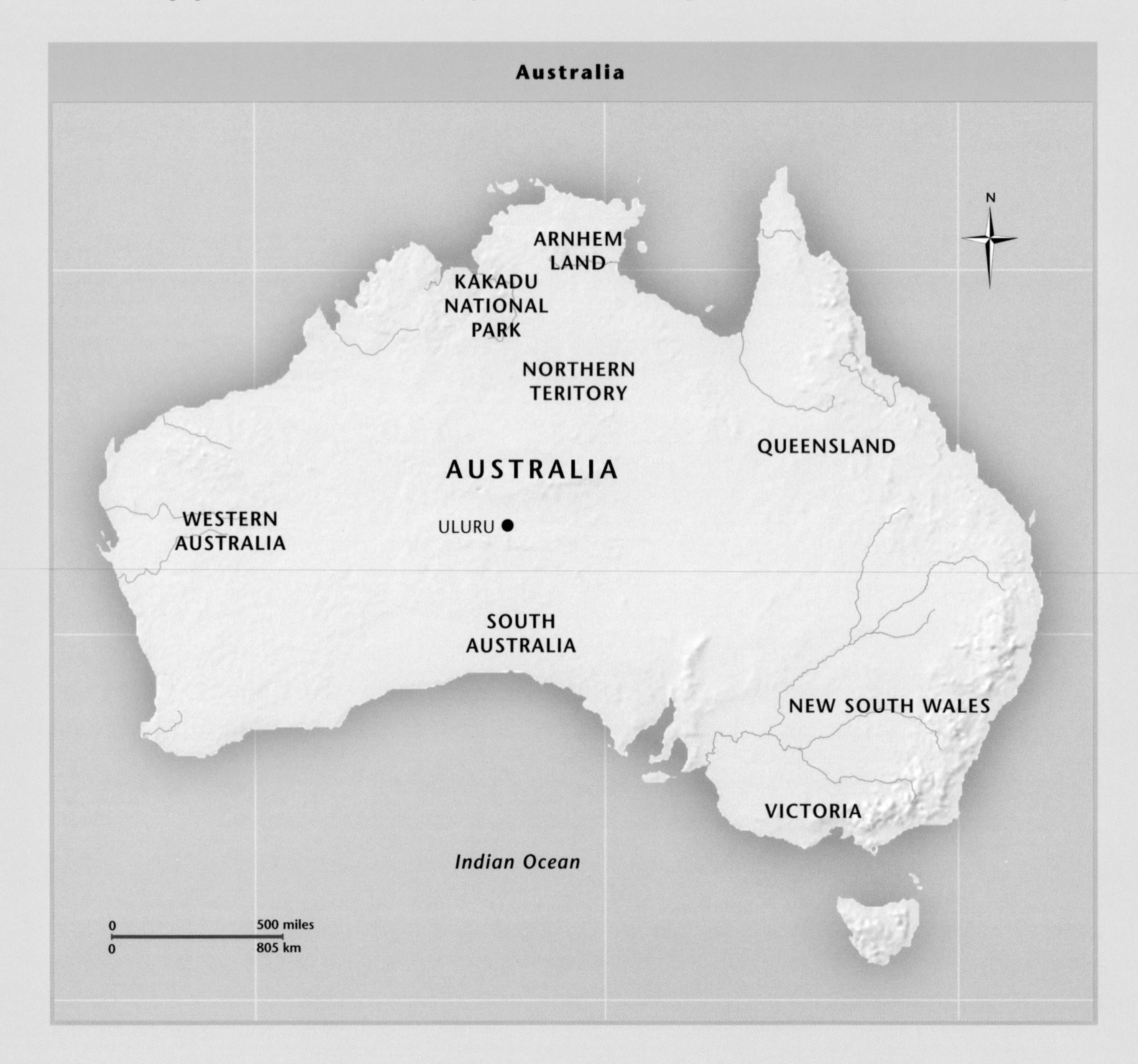

Right: *The bodies of these boys are decorated for ceremonies that admit them into adulthood.*

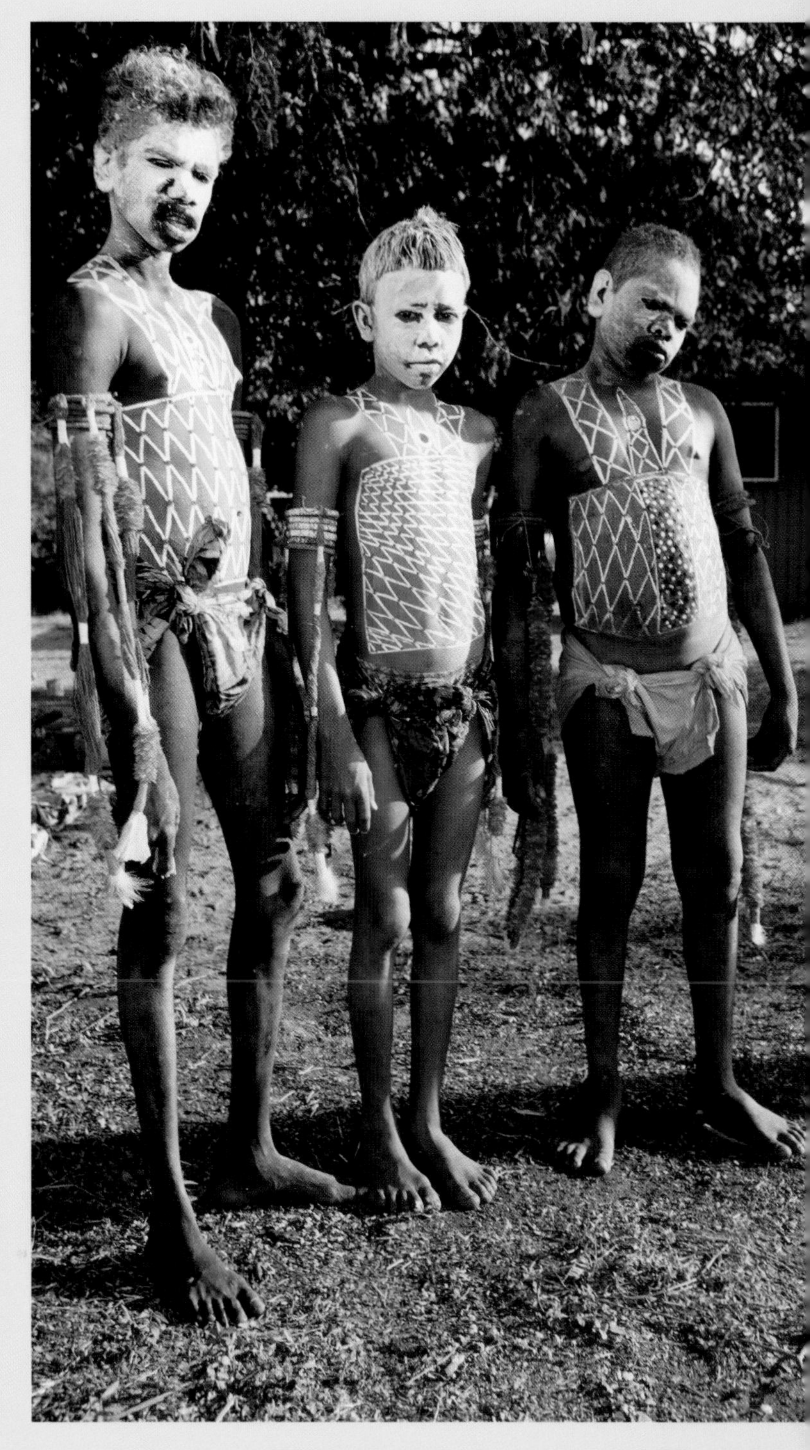

ancestors of the Crocodile people. The groups of people who identify with totemic ancestors are often smaller than language groups. In many regions, totem groups form associations with other groups and perform ceremonies together. In most parts of Australia, Aborigines become members of the totemic group of their father. However, in some regions membership of a totem group is inherited through the mother.

Myths, ceremonies, and places

The doctrines or beliefs of Aboriginal peoples are recorded in the form of myths, rituals, or ceremonies that reenact the events described in the myths, focus attention on the sacred places where those events happened, and recall the religious laws that govern how Aboriginals treat each other and how they should conduct their daily lives.

Because Aboriginal people did not have writing before British settlement in Australia, the myths were handed down from generation to generation in an oral tradition. People of each group told many myths, including moral tales and creation stories.

Rituals or ceremonies include songs and dances that reenact the events recorded in the myths. Dancers mimic the actions of totemic ancestors, such as animals, birds, and fish. Songs recount ancestral events and evoke places and creatures connected with the ancestors. Designs painted in ochers (red, yellow, white, and black) on participants' bodies and on sacred objects, or drawn on the ground, represent the ancestors and the places associated with them.

People perform ceremonies for many reasons. Some mark a particular stage in a person's life: the occasion of a girl's first menstruation, a boy's initiation into manhood, marriage, or a person's death and burial. Other rituals include dances performed by men preparing to fight, or a ceremony performed to make peace between warring groups. Some ceremonies have a magical purpose, such as to bring the rains, encourage fish to breed, or attract a lover. People of different regions come together at certain ceremonies to exchange goods. Many ceremonies have secret aspects in which older men reveal sacred dances and objects to younger men. In some regions women have secret ceremonies of their own. People believe that the elements of a ceremony—the songs, designs, and sacred objects—are filled with the power of the ancestors, which people can harness for their benefit, or sometimes for aggressive purposes in order to harm enemies.

Sacred places are associated with totemic ancestors. Each creator ancestor was believed to have left marks in particular places in the forms of rocks, gullies, colors in the earth, rivers, water holes, and trees, or on the coast, in reefs and sandbanks. A certain rock was the backbone of the Shark ancestor, for example, or a group of rocks was thought to be the remains of Emu, which was killed by Dingo. The group of people believed to be descended from the ancestor spirit—the totemic group—owns the places connected with that ancestor.

Above: Paintings on rocks depict creation myths, sacred sites, or ceremonies that can only be performed by particular totem groups.

Aboriginal people believed that the totemic ancestors gave them their laws. These include whom a person can and cannot marry, how people should behave toward the elders, how relatives of various kinds ought to behave toward one another, and the ownership of land and waters. Local groups who cooperate in performing major ceremonies, such as the initiation of boys, agree in principle to a common set of laws set down by their totemic ancestors. Unlike the doctrines of many religions, Aboriginal mythologies do not divide mythological beings into those that are wholly good and wholly evil. Creator ancestors include beings that had both good and bad, dangerous and life-giving aspects. Among the more dangerous beings were the so-called Rainbow Serpents, believed to live deep in water holes, freshwater lakes, and rivers. These serpents were associated with thunderstorms, lightning, and the rainbow.

Unlike followers of most religions, Aboriginal people do not worship gods and goddesses. Instead they reenact the ancestral past and, in so doing, tap into ancestral powers to regenerate and sustain life.

Myths of morality

Aboriginal myths have many purposes, not all of them serious. Some myths are stories told to warn children—such as that of the monster who comes to carry off a child who cries too much. Others are moral tales that make their point by describing the disastrous consequences of a breach of obligations to relatives. They often combine "just so" stories that tell how it was that the stork came to fly, or how the echidna got its spines. Typically these stories begin with a dispute or wrongdoing and end in the transformation of the ancestors into animals, birds, or other kinds of beings.

One example of this type of myth is the story of Jabiru (a type of stork) and Emu (see box, opposite). In this myth, told by Yolngu people of Arnhem Land, in Northern Territory, Emu is Jabiru's wife's father. The story is about the duty of a daughter's husband to provide for his wife's father. It hinges on the need to include sufficient fatty food in the diet. Like many hunters and gatherers, Yolngu prize fatty meat or fish. They do not eat meat without sufficient fat.

Creation myths

The more important myths concern the creation of places, peoples, ceremonies, and laws. Older people would tell creation stories to younger people, gradually revealing more secret aspects. Creation myths were also told to adults visiting their land and group for the first time, either as fireside stories or to explain the meaning of a ceremony, painting, song, or dance.

Such myths recount events that took place during the creative era long, long ago: the Dreamtime. This name reflects beliefs that people could gain knowledge of the ancestors and ancestral events in dreams. According to Aboriginal beliefs, the ancestor spirits also created the landscape and the animals and plants in their dreams.

While most creator ancestors were nonhuman mammals, reptiles, birds, or fish, some of these spirits had a human form. In one story told by the Murring people of the southeast coast of New South Wales, a human is the principal character. The story relates how a man named Daramulun lived with Ngalalbal, his mother. At that time the world was as featureless as the sky and hard as stone. The land extended far out across what is now the sea. Then Kaboka, the thrush, caused a great flood that covered the whole country. Animals, birds, and reptiles survived, but the only people to remain were those who had crawled out of the water on to Mount Dromedary. Daramulun restored the land, planted trees, and gave the Yuin people their laws. Then he went up into the sky, where he now lives and watches over people. To this day the elders hand down his laws from father to child.

As well as the creator ancestors, Aboriginal mythologies include many other kinds of spirit beings. Each person is thought to have a number of spirits or souls. Trickster spirits inhabit the forest, where, if encountered, they make people confused and lost. Spirits of winds cause illness, while spirits of caves pull people in and kill them. In Arnhem Land, in the Northern Territory, people tell of mimih spirits, who live in a world parallel to the human world inside the rocks of that rugged region.

One myth tells how the mimih spirits live in the rocks. They are so skinny that they have to shelter in caves from the strong winds, which might break their long bodies and necks. In former times, people could not see the mimih and did not mix with them—the spirits lived in the rocks while people lived in their camps. There are many rock paintings of mimih spirits in the country of the Kunwinjku people of Arnhem Land, but the mimih are said to have painted these images themselves. Mimih spirits taught the Kunwinjku people their songs and dances long ago and instructed them how to hunt kangaroos. The Kunwinjku still sing, dance, and hunt the same way.

The Story of Jabiru and Emu

Jabiru (the black-necked stork) and his wife, Emu's daughter, went out in a canoe and speared lots of fish. When they got back to shore, Jabiru ate all the best, fatty parts of the stingray fish they had caught, leaving only the lean meat. Emu's daughter pointed out that Jabiru had left none of the best part of the fish for her father, saying, "He is not a dog. He cannot be treated this way." But Jabiru said that, as he had caught them, the fish belonged to him. When they returned to camp, Emu discovered that Jabiru had eaten all the best parts of the fish. He became very angry and hit Jabiru with a club. In return, Jabiru broke Emu's wing with his club. That is why emus can only walk now and not fly. Jabiru walked around until he found a round stone, just like an emu's egg. He threw it at Emu and it went right inside him. Emu thought, "That is my egg. I shall keep it from now on." Jabiru flew high into the sky. Emu attached a spear to his spear-thrower, threw it, and hit Jabiru in the buttocks. Jabiru fell into a salt marsh, where he rested for a time and said, "This is my water, I shall wade in it." The spear went right through him and came out of his mouth. It became his long beak with which to spear fish in the water. Emu swore never to go near the water again, and to live in the forest.

This moral tale tells of the disastrous consequences of a son-in-law failing in his duty to his wife's father. It is also a just-so story, for it tells how it came about that emus live in the forest and cannot fly, while jabirus wade and catch fish in the salt marshes near the sea. The male emu's acquisition of an egg in the story reflects the fact that male emus sit on and hatch the eggs.

Right: *The jabiru, or black-necked stork, is associated with myth.*

Aboriginal people believe that dangerous ghosts of the dead haunt the living and make them sick. Other spirits of the deceased travel to a distant land of the dead or, according to the beliefs of some regions, return to the waters of a person's homeland—where that individual came from at the time of their conception. The types of such beings vary greatly from district to district.

Below: This Aboriginal painting depicts rainbow serpents, powerful beings that were said to inhabit lakes, rivers, and water holes.

Myths and places

Many Aboriginal myths recount how particular places came to have unique features. During a visit to that place, people take the opportunity to tell its story.

There are places of great significance to Aboriginal people throughout Australia. Rocks, lagoons, creeks and rivers, hills and reefs, even particular trees, are regarded as the traces of the ancestors and are filled with their power. This power makes some of these places very dangerous, so only older people can visit them. Only old men can visit some sites, while others are restricted to women. Other places associated with myths include the sky—clouds, sun, moon, and stars—as well as the thunderstorms and lightning.

According to a story told by Kunai people, for example, Dingo turned people into stone for refusing to share food with him. In this myth, the event occurred at Metung, in eastern Victoria, where one of the stones still stands. The freshwater springs that bubble up through mud and shallow seawater on the Arnhem Land coast were created by the Djang'kawu, who thrust their long digging sticks into the ground. At a large outcrop of rock in what is now Kakadu National Park, in the Northern Territory, Namorrodo cruelly sealed a group of people inside a cave and left a sign in the form of a red spot on the rock.

Some stories relate how it was that a man became the moon, destined to die and be reborn forever, unlike humans, who are mortal. Myths of southeastern Australia tell how Emu became the dark patch in the Milky Way, visible in southern skies and known, in English, as the Woolsack. Other Aborginal myths tell of the creation of the stars of the Southern Cross (see box, page 200).

Tracks across the desert

Many myths tell of the long journeys of totemic ancestors that link places, sometimes across vast distances. Long, often invisible, mythical tracks crisscross the deserts of Western Australia. These tracks mark the long journeys of many totemic ancestors in the mythologies of the peoples of those regions. In the northern part of the Western Desert, stories about the Tingari men follow their long journey from place to place. For example, one myth tells of Native Cat's reaction to a breach of the rights of landowners. Walking near his home at Lake Macdonald, he came across a piece of emu fat and noticed the tracks left by the Tingari men. Native Cat deduced that the men had speared an emu to the east of the lake at a place called Tikartikanya and cooked the bird. This made Native Cat angry, because the men had sneaked into his country without permission and had not shared the meat with him. Native Cat told his sons that he was going to catch the men and bring them back. He set off toward the west, following the tracks of the Tingari men, who had by that time turned into wild dogs. On the way, Native Cat passed the Possum people among the clay pans at Yiitjuruny. His journey, and the mythical track, continued toward the west.

Right: *This cave painting depicts the Wandjina spirit, which is said to have disappeared into the ground after creating the landscape of an area.*

The ownership of places

Australia was divided into named areas, from a few square miles on the coast to thousands of square miles in the desert. Each area, together with its ancestral places, myths, and ceremonies, belonged to a particular Aboriginal group, and in many regions this traditional ownership of country continues. In many parts of Australia a person becomes a member of a parent's group, while in other places, such as many parts of the desert, a person belongs to the area and group where he or she was born or

conceived. In all regions, people have rights to hunt, gather vegetable foods, and fish not only in their own country but also in areas to which they are connected in a variety of ways.

These links include the country of an individual's mother's, grandparent's, and spouse's groups. Where long ancestral journeys connect many places, a person who belongs to one place on the route also has some claim over other places along the same ancestral track.

Myths, ceremonies, and art

Not only do myths tell how features of the landscape came into being, but they also explain the meaning of songs, dances, and designs that depict and reenact events involving the ancestors and other beings.

Dancers perform in the role of ancestor spirits, identifying with them by their actions and decoration. Aboriginal singers sing in the first person, as if it is the ancestor singing about him- or herself. Sometimes people perform a ceremony at the actual place where the event was supposed to have happened. These events could also be reenacted elsewhere, but the reenactment would not be considered to have the same force.

The Creation of the Southern Cross

The origins of the constellation known in English as the Southern Cross are recorded in the myths of more than one group of Aboriginal people.

In one story, from Western Australia, a group of people traveled a long distance, then camped at dusk near some trees. The nearest water hole was far away. Some of the girls in the group were given large pieces of bark to collect water for the children. On the way back, the girls lingered, played, and wasted the water.

When it was getting late, the men of the group went to look for them and found the girls still playing. The men grew frustrated and angry because the girls were ignoring them. The men prodded the girls on the calves with their spears. The girls ran away, and as they ran a huge wind blew them into the sky. The men threw their spears at them, but the girls scattered to avoid the spears.

As a result, the stars of the Southern Cross constellation are scattered. However, these stars always stay in the same place in the sky, because the girls are afraid to come back to Earth for fear of being speared.

Below: The origin of the stars of the Southern Cross was explained in a famous Aboriginal myth.

Above: Australia's Western Desert is crossed by ancestral tracks that link sacred Aboriginal places.

Much of the Aboriginal art seen in galleries of major cities such as New York and London, England, comes from paintings made during ceremonies. These pictures are painted on sacred objects or in caves in the form of sand drawings, made in colored sand and earth on the ground.

Many of the designs depict the totemic ancestors, the places they created, the ceremonies they performed, and sacred objects they made and left in the ground. Because these pictures are often geometric (or abstract), rather than depicting figures of people and animals, it requires special knowledge to interpret them.

Variation in Aboriginal mythologies

Although they have some common features, Aboriginal religions and their mythologies vary greatly from place to place. In the Western Desert, for example, long ancestral tracks link each important place (a water hole or a group of rocks) with many others. Many of the ceremonies performed in this region seek to enhance the number of food animals and plants by tapping ancestral power.

In southeast Australia, people believed that the original creator, which each group named differently, went up into the sky after traveling across the country with his family. These creator spirits left traces of their activities at many places in the form of rocks, water holes, and trees. For example, stone fish traps in the Darling River near what is now the town of Brewarrina in New South Wales were said to have been made by the sons of Byamee, the sky being. This sky ancestor linked many peoples across a wide region.

In Kimberley, northern Australia, the mythology is dominated by giant pythons or other snakes, believed to live deep in freshwater pools. The spirit of each person is thought to come from these pools at the time of conception. In much of Australia, people credit Rainbow Serpents with creating summer storms and cyclones (hurricanes). They are both a source of life and extremely dangerous: if offended, the Rainbow Serpents can cause great disasters.

IAN KEEN

Bibliography

Berndt, R. M., and C. H. Berndt. *The Speaking Land: Myth and Story in Aboriginal Australia.* Rochester, VT: Inner Traditions, 1994.

Nganjmirra, Nawakadj. *Kunwinjku Spirit.* Melbourne: Melbourne University Press, 1997.

SEE ALSO: Ancestor Worship; Animals; Animism; Death and the Afterlife; Moon; Mystery Cults; Stars; Sun.

AZTECS

The Aztecs were a warlike people who frequently subjugated smaller groups in central Mexico, partly to obtain victims for human sacrifice. Many of their myths reflected their violent culture. At the same time, however, they created a highly sophisticated empire and built impressive pyramids and temples.

The Aztecs were a Nahuatl-speaking people who, historians believe, originally came from northern Mexico and settled in central Mexico during the early 14th century. They built Tenochtitlán, the largest city in Mesoamerica, which today forms the foundation for Mexico City. The city, which by the early 16th century spanned 5 square miles (13 sq km), was the center of a vast empire that ruled between 5 and 6 million people in central and southern Mexico.

Despite the empire's enormous size, military successes, and economic security, it ended in 1521 when Spanish troops, relying on a coalition of native groups hostile toward the Aztecs, blockaded Tenochtitlán, causing many of its inhabitants to starve or die of disease. With the fall of Tenochtitlán and the capitulation of the last Aztec emperor, Cuauhtémoc, the sophisticated culture and complex belief system of the Aztecs also collapsed. It was supplanted by Christianity as taught or enforced by Spanish missionaries.

Although the Aztec civilization was less than two centuries old by the time it ceased, it was based on a millennium of rich cultures and belief systems that had previously thrived in the region. Much like the Romans, who adopted mythologies from the Greeks and Etruscans, the Aztecs borrowed deities, myths, and religious practices from the Olmecs, Zapotecs, and Toltecs, among others. From the Maya, an equally sophisticated but older people who lived

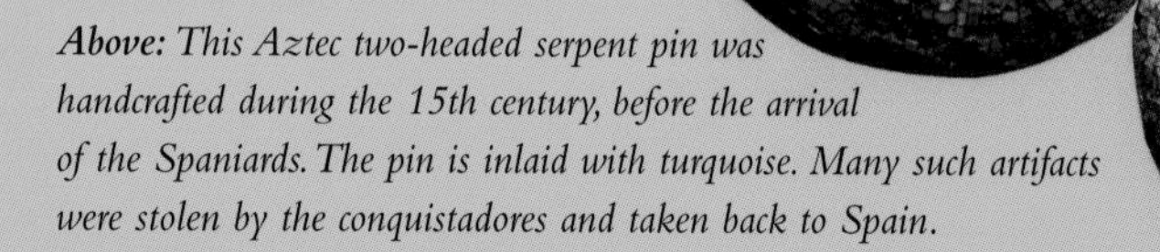

***Above:** This Aztec two-headed serpent pin was handcrafted during the 15th century, before the arrival of the Spaniards. The pin is inlaid with turquoise. Many such artifacts were stolen by the conquistadores and taken back to Spain.*

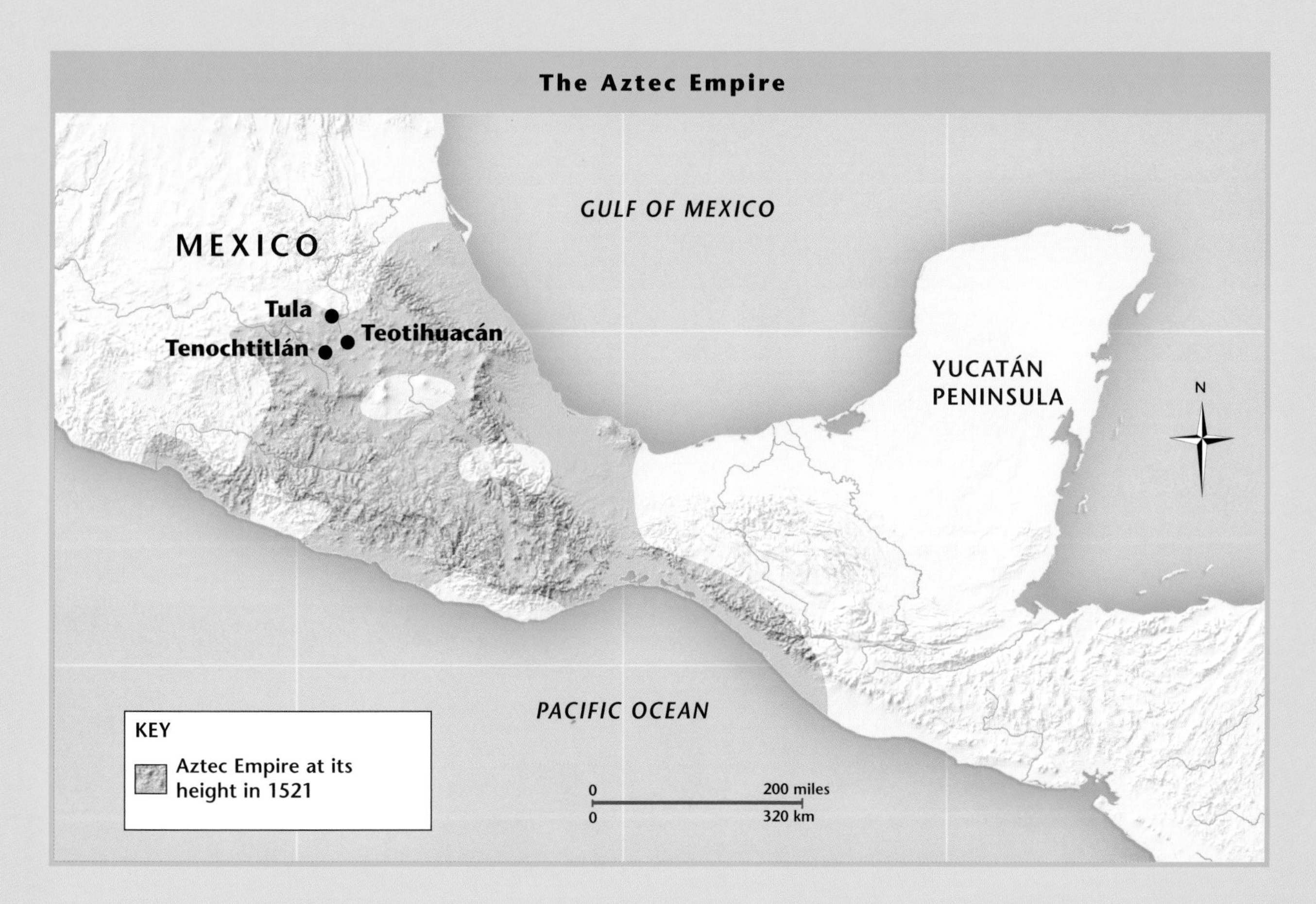

(and still do) in the Yucatán Peninsula, the Aztecs adapted their complicated calendar. Basically the calendar was made up of a solar year of 365 days that ran concurrently with a sacred year of 260 days, together forming a larger cycle of 52 years.

Founding of the capital

The Aztecs viewed their world as part of an endless cycle of destruction and regeneration, and their mythologies reflected this. When the Spaniards first encountered the Aztecs, they found a people whose religion and myths were central to their lives. Tenochtitlán itself was also seen as sacred, and the city was founded, according to one legend, by guidance from Huitzilopochtli, a chief deity and god of war. When the Aztecs were migrating from northern Mexico, Huitzilopochtli appeared in a vision to one of his priests. He instructed the priest that the Aztecs should build a mighty city on the spot where an eagle was seen perching on a large cactus. The following morning just such a scene was discovered on some marshland near a lake. To mark the site the Aztecs built a temporary temple to honor the god; over the years they constructed Tenochtitlán in the same place. By the 16th century Tenochtitlán was a well-planned metropolis with canals, roads, palaces, and pyramids, including the Great Pyramid in the city center dedicated to two gods, Huitzilopochtli and Tlaloc. It was on this pyramid that most human sacrifices took place.

Aztec religious belief system

The Aztecs had a pantheistic belief system that included many deities, most of whom controlled or affected the harvests and weather. However, their four primary gods were believed to have been brothers, sons of the creator Ometeotl. These were Huitzilopochtli, god of war; Tezcatlipoca, the "Smoking Mirror"; Xipe Totec, god of agriculture; and Quetzalcoatl, the feathered serpent. Other important deities included Tonatiuh, god of the sun, and Tlaloc, god of rain (see box, page 205).

Leading the worship of the deities were the priests, who were also responsible for performing the many rituals that were an important part of Aztec life. From celebrating a birth to ensuring heavenly intervention for a good harvest, the priests were heavily involved in almost every area of Aztec culture. They supervised all religious, educational, and artistic aspects of the empire. They governed the schools and oversaw the public rites and religious rituals. However, although the priests were the empire's interlocutors with the gods, the emperor, who was seen as divine himself, ruled over them.

When the army of Hernan Cortés (1485–1547) first saw Aztec priests, one Spaniard wrote: "They wore black cloaks like cassocks and long gowns reaching to their feet. Some had hoods like those worn by canons, and others had smaller hoods like those of Dominicans, and they wore their hair very long, right down to the waist, and some had it even reaching down to the ankles. The hair was covered with blood, and so matted together that it could not be separated, and their ears were cut to pieces by way of penance. They stank like sulfur and they had another bad smell like carrion. They were sons of chiefs and abstained from women. They fasted on certain days and what I saw them eat was the pith of seeds. Their fingernails were very long, and we heard it said that these priests were very pious and led good lives." Historians now suspect that the Spaniard who made the observation, named Bernal Diaz del Castillo, had actually witnessed the priests during a special period of penance and the description may not have been typical.

Human sacrifice

The most important function the priests had was to satisfy the Aztec gods, and this was done primarily through the ritual of human sacrifice. The sacrifices were originally carried out on a modest scale. However, as the Aztec nation grew more powerful, more sacrifices were needed to keep the favor of the gods. At the dedication of the great pyramid in Tenochtitlán, 20,000 captives were killed.

Right: *The legend of the founding of the Aztec capital Tenochtitlán is depicted on this illustration. The eagle perched on a cactus was the sign from the god Huitzilopochtli that the Aztecs were to build their capital city on the spot.*

Major Aztec Deities

Chalchiuhtlicue: "She of the Jade Skirt"; goddess of springs, rivers, lakes, and the sea.
Coatlicue: "She of the Serpent Skirt"; goddess mother of fire, Huitzilopochtli, Coyolxauhqui, and 400 other male deities.
Coyolxauhqui: Warrior sister of Huitzilopochtli.
Huehueteotl: "Old Deity"; god of fire.
Huitzilopochtli: God of war. His birth has similarities with the birth of the Greek goddess of war, Athena.
Metztli: The moon, formerly Tecciztecatl.
Mictlantecuhtli: God of the underworld.
Mixcoatl: God of the hunt.
Ometeotl: Supreme being, creator of the gods; also known as Tonacatecuhtli and Tonacacihuatl.
Popocatepetl: "Smoke Mountain"; god of sacred mountains.
Quetzalcoatl: "Feathered Serpent"; one of the chief deities who was god of wisdom, learning, writing, and books, as well as the symbol of death and resurrection.
Tezcatlipoca: "Smoking Mirror"; often characterized as the most powerful supreme deity. His major emblem was an obsidian mirror.
Tlaloc: God of rain.
Tonatiuh: The sun god, formerly Nanauatzin. His emblem was the solar disk, often worn on the back of the priests who impersonated him during rituals. Aztec warriors were responsible for providing the sun with human sacrifices.
Xipe Totec: God of agriculture and especially crop seeds.
Xiuhtecuhtli: A fire god.
Xochipilli: God of music, dance, and flowers; comparable to the Greek deity of wine, Dionysus.

Although human sacrifice was commonplace in Aztec society, most of the victims were prisoners of war. Sometimes wars were arranged with enemy groups for the sole purpose of obtaining sacrificial victims. During the sacrifice ritual the prisoner would mount the steps of a pyramid, such as the Great Pyramid in Tenochtitlán. At the top he or she would lie on an altar and the priest would puncture the victim's chest with a razor-sharp obsidian knife. In the same movement the priest would rip out the still-beating heart and offer it to one of the gods, usually Tonatiuh, the sun god.

The origin of human sacrifice lay in Aztec mythology. One myth explained that the world was created by Quetzalcoatl and Tezcatlipoca when they tore in two the earth monster Tlaltecuhtli. The upper half of its body became the sky and the lower half the earth. However, after the transformation Tlaltecuhtli would only allow crops to grow if it was fed human blood.

Another myth offered an alternative

Right: This stone statue depicts Xochipilli, the god of flowers, music, and dance. Originally, the figure would have held a rattle in each hand.

explanation for the practice of human sacrifice. The myth said that in order to create the present world a deity had to be sacrificed on a special pyre. First the vain god Tecciztecatl volunteered to be burned and therefore be made into the sun. However, in the end it was the more self-effacing god Nanauatzin who won the honor. Nanauatzin jumped onto the burning pyre and shortly thereafter rose to become the mighty sun god Tonatiuh. Tecciztecatl was immediately jealous and he too ran into the fire, but instead of emerging as another sun, he rose to become the moon.

Tonatiuh, blazing in glory but not satisfied, refused to move across the sky unless he was fed with the hearts and blood of the other deities, who had no choice but to acquiesce to the powerful god's demands. Therefore the Aztec priests believed that they too had to offer human hearts and blood to Tonatiuh in order to keep the sun moving across the sky.

Below: *An Aztec mask worn during sacrificial rituals. The mask is made from a human skull. In place of the nose is an obsidian knife.*

Ometeotl the Creator

In Aztec mythology the supreme creator was Ometeotl. Despite his important position in the Aztec pantheon, Ometeotl was not widely worshiped, nor were there any major rituals or celebrations dedicated to him. Like many Mesoamerican deities, Ometeotl was both male and female, and sometimes he was depicted as two different deities, Tonacatecuhtli (male) and Tonacacihuatl (female), who were locked in a permanent sexual embrace. Ometeotl created the world with his breath, and then created the other gods. His universe included, depending on the versions, 13 or 9 layers of heaven and the same number for the underworld. The world the Aztecs existed in was believed to have been shaped like an oval. At the horizon the sea curved up to become the sky, forming a dome over the earth. This was not the only explanation for the world's existence. Another myth said that the earth was an alligator swimming in a vast sea and the undulating shape of its back formed the mountains and valleys of Mexico.

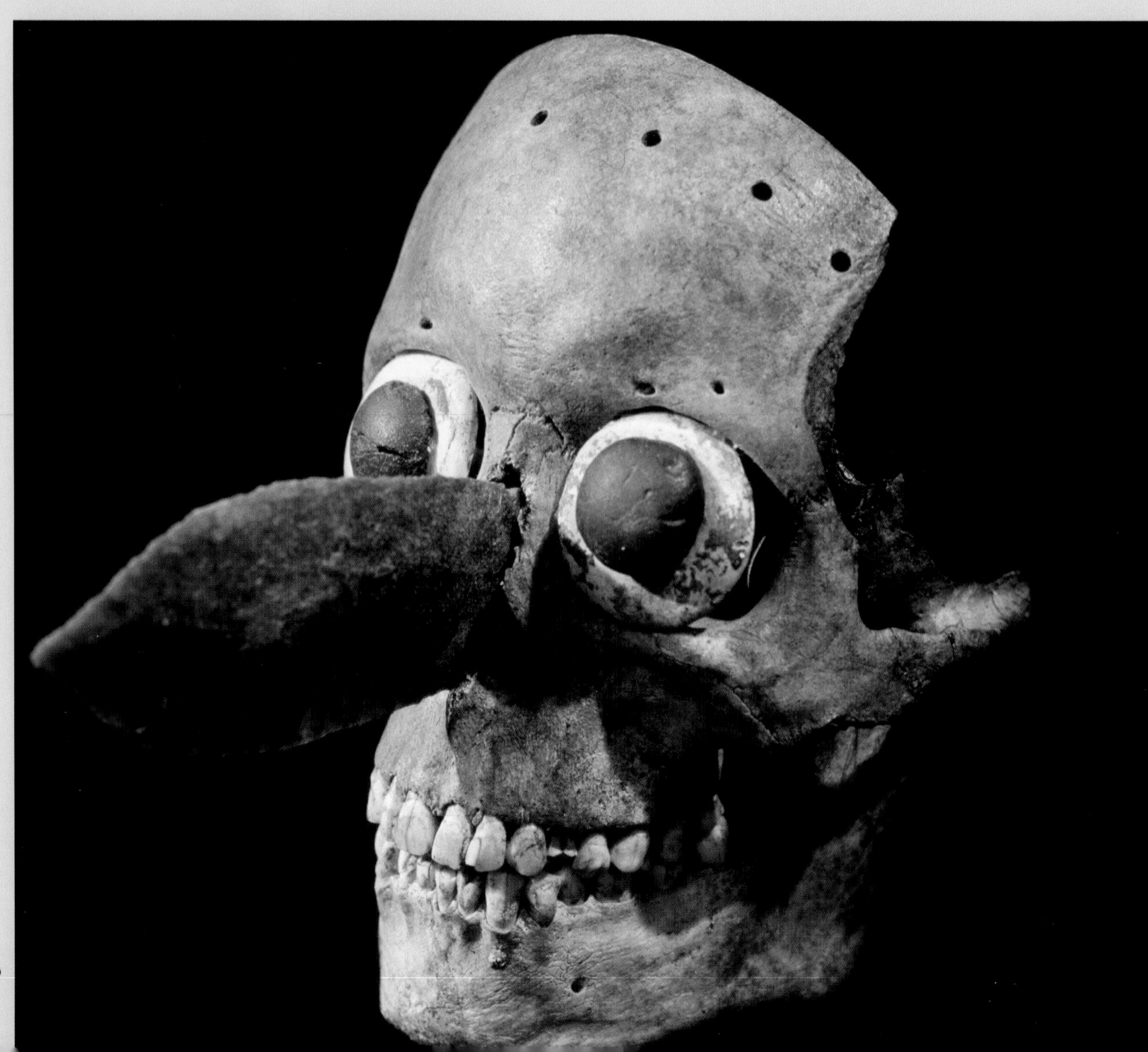

Huitzilopochtli and Coatlicue

The war god Huitzilopochtli appears to have been an original Aztec god, rather than one borrowed from a neighboring culture. Associated with the sun, he had attributes similar to those of other deities, such as Tezcatlipoca, Mixcoatl, and Xiuhtecuhtli (see box, page 205). It is doubtful that he had a widespread or enthusiastic following beyond the Valley of Mexico, where the Aztec capital Tenochtitlán lay. In fact, representations of him were rare elsewhere in Mesoamerica.

Scholars have discovered various accounts of the origin of Huitzilopochtli, but in many versions, his birth occurred at Coatepetl ("Serpent Mountain"), a mountain located near the ancient city of Tula, north of Mexico City and near Teotihuacán, a vast city of Mesoamerican antiquity that already lay in ruins by the time the Aztecs arrived in the region. According to Spanish chroniclers, the Aztecs traveled to Coatepetl annually to celebrate a great feast in honor of Huitzilopochtli.

Another wholly Aztec creation was Coatlicue, the mother of Huitzilopochtli. Coatlicue was also known as "She of the Serpent Skirt," because the Aztecs believed she wore a skirt of intertwined snakes. Coatlicue was a version of the Earth Mother, and despite having given birth to Huitzilopochtli, Coyolxauhqui, and 400 sons, she was considered by the Aztecs to have been a virgin. When the Spanish Catholic

Sources of Aztec Mythology

Above: The Codex Fejérváry-Mayer, one of the most important Aztec codices. Historians believe that the codex's paintings depict scenes from the lives of Aztec merchants.

Although the Aztecs did not use writing, they did use codices with pictographs. A codex is similar to a book in that it is made up of pieces of parchment or pages sewn or bound together. Many ancient civilizations used codices, and historians believe that the Aztecs started using them around 1000 CE, long before they moved to central Mexico. The Aztec codices were used mainly by priests to make astrological predictions and to record royal history. They were also used by government officials for administrative accounts such as tax or tribute collecting. Although the conquering Spaniards destroyed much of the Aztecs' existing culture and historical records, some codices survived. These include the Vienna Codex, the Codex Colombino, and the Codex Fejérváry-Mayer, all made before 1350.

Other historical sources have come from a few Spaniards who, during the early years of colonization, learned the Aztec language, Nahuatl, in order to chronicle the Aztecs' history and culture. These early Spanish chroniclers include missionaries Toribio de Benavente, Bernardino de Sahagún, and Diego Duran. Sahagún's interest in the indigenous peoples was both religious and anthropological. He studied their culture, plants, medicine, language and mythology, comparing the latter to European myths, and recorded his findings in a massive four-volume work called *The General History of the Things of New Spain.*

Above: This eagle-shaped stone container was used as a receptacle for the hearts of the Aztecs' sacrificial victims.

missionaries were converting the Aztecs, they tried to link the goddess to the Virgin Mary to ease the transition to Christianity. The miraculous appearance of the Virgin of Guadalupe to an Aztec in 1531 on a site sacred to Coatlicue prompted millions of Aztecs to convert to Catholicism.

In Aztec mythology the Earth Mother was typical of Mesoamerican predecessors—a generic deity who took on many different forms and identities and was known by several names, including Tonantzin, Teteoinnan, Toci, Yohualticitl, and Xochiquetzal.

Coyolxauhqui versus Huitzilopochtli

Coyolxauhqui was the half sister of Huitzilopochtli. She appears to have been originally a fire goddess worshiped in central Mexico. Her name means "painted with bells," and in depictions of her Coyolxauhqui wore bells on her cheeks. The myth of Huitzilopochtli's birth, which featured Coyolxauhqui, was one of the most important stories of Aztec mythology. The following version is based on the one recorded by the Spanish chronicler Sahagún.

One day Coatlicue, the mother of the warrior goddess Coyolxauhqui and of 400 other male warrior deities, was performing her domestic chores when a ball of feathers fell from the sky. She tucked the ball in her waistband and carried on with her tasks. Later she discovered that the ball had impregnated her. As her womb swelled and she grew more obviously pregnant, Coyolxauhqui became angered and ashamed because of the child her mother was carrying. Coyolxauhqui convinced her brothers that their mother had to be killed. The news of the plot terrified Coatlicue, but the child in her womb, Huitzilopochtli, reassured her not to worry.

When he was born, Huitzilopochtli arrived fully armed and brandishing a special knife. Immediately he fought Coyolxauhqui and killed her. He dismembered her body and threw the pieces to the bottom of Coatepetl. At the defeat of Coyolxauhqui, the 400 brothers fled.

The Five Suns

According to Aztec mythology, four worlds or ages, known as Suns, had existed before the one in which they lived, and each had been destroyed by a divinely inflicted catastrophe. Each of the Suns was ruled by a specific deity and was associated with a particular element. The First Sun was associated with earth and was ruled over by Tezcatlipoca, the most powerful son of Tonacatecuhtli and Tonacacihuatl. During the First Sun it was believed that the world was populated by a race of giants. It ended when Quetzalcoatl struck Tezcatlipoca, causing him to fall into the waters. He then turned into a jaguar and ate the giants.

Quetzalcoatl governed the Second Sun, and it was ended when an enormous hurricane swept over the world, destroying nearly everything. The Third Sun was ruled by Tlaloc, and it was during this age that farming began. Quetzalcoatl brought an end to the Third Sun when he caused rainy ash to consume the world. Tlaloc's wife, the goddess Chalchiuhtlicue, created and ruled over the Fourth Sun, but then destroyed it by releasing a global flood.

The Fifth Sun—the age of the Aztecs—was ruled over by Tonatiuh. The Aztecs believed that this age too would end in a series of violent earthquakes. Although the apocalypse was inevitable, they believed it could be postponed by feeding Tonatiuh sacrifices of human hearts and blood.

Right: *This statue depicts the sun god Tonatiuh, whose age would end with a violent earthquake. The Aztec symbol for an earthquake is engraved on his back.*

In 1978 a stone relief of Coyolxauhqui was discovered at a Tenochtitlán excavation site. Archaeologists determined that it had stood at the base of the steps beneath Huitzilopochtli's shrine on the Great Pyramid. During the Aztec era the fresh corpse of each sacrificial victim would have been thrown down the steps of the pyramid to land on the stone as a reenactment of the killing of Coyolxauhqui at Coatepetl. According to Sahagún, the warriors who had captured the prisoners were given an arm or a thigh from the victim to take home for a ceremonial banquet. The human limb would have been cooked in a special stew with chilis and tomato and served in solemn reverence.

Huitzilopochtli's birth was important to the Aztecs for another reason, too. As the god of war, he symbolized the importance the Aztecs placed in military strength. In other words, just as Huitzilopochtli triumphed over Coyolxauhqui and the 400 brothers, so the Aztecs believed they would triumph over their enemies.

BLAISE STAPLES

Bibliography

Ferguson, Diana. *Tales of the Plumed Serpent: Aztec, Inca and Mayan Myths.* New York: Sterling, 2000.

Taube, Karl. *Aztec and Maya Myths.* Austin, TX: University of Texas Press, 1993.

SEE ALSO: Apocalypse Myths; Blood; Calendar; Creation Myths; Earth Mother; Flood Myths; Maya; Moon; Olmecs; Quetzalcoatl; Sacrifice; Sun; Tlaloc.

BAAL

Baal was a Phoenician and Canaanite fertility god who was worshiped in different ways in various West Asian towns and villages. The name of Baal also figures in the Old Testament of the Bible and was used by the Israelites to signify any false god.

Baal was one of the gods worshiped by the Canaanites who lived along the eastern shores of the Mediterranean Sea in modern-day Palestine, Israel, and Syria as early 3000 BCE. He was later adopted by the Phoenicians, who lived in the area now known as Lebanon from around 1000 BCE. Baal was most commonly known as the storm god, the source of rain and dew that watered crops, and was therefore seen as essential to the survival of the ancient Canaanites and Phoenicians. Baal was the most widely worshiped deity in Canaan, although he was not the chief god, who was El. Different rituals were associated with Baal in different cities, including sacrifices, prayers, and perhaps sacred prostitution, orgies, and human sacrifice.

Uncovering Baal

Until the early 20th century little was known about how Baal was worshiped or how he was represented, and scholars relied mostly on the Bible (see box, page 214) for mythological and sociological speculation. Then in the 1920s archaeologists discovered the Canaanite city of Ugarit, modern Ras Shamra in northern Syria (see box, page 213). Among the ruins there archaeologists found clay

Below: *This temple to Baal was built at Palmyra, now known as Tadmur, in Syria in 17 CE on a site where temples had stood for over 1,500 years. Construction continued on it for over 200 years.*

Above: *This statuette of Baal from the 14th century BCE shows a distinctly Egyptian influence. His gold crown is similar to the crowns worn by the kings of Egypt. Baal was accepted by the Egyptians at this time, alongside their other deities.*

Above: Mount Saphon, near Ugarit, is the traditional home of Baal. It is now an arid area, but 4,000 years ago there was higher rainfall.

The Canaanite Gods

Among the writings found at Ugarit are three records listing 33 or 34 gods who were worshiped by the Canaanites. Although Baal was the most prominent god in the mythologies, other gods were more powerful.

The chief god was El, who was father of the gods. He may have been thought of as the creator of the world. His consort was Asherah, mother of the gods, whom he treated with respect and consulted in all matters. Anat was Baal's consort and was portrayed in the myths as a violent goddess of sexual love and war. Anat and Asherah are often considered to be the same person as the goddess Astarte. Baal's chief adversaries were Yam, the goddess of the sea, and Mot, the god of the underworld and drought in the land. Another god of importance was Kothar, the god of crafts. He was a master builder and weapon maker.

The Canaanite gods were depicted in human form, and it was believed that they had similar longings, desires, and appetites as humans. However, the myths portrayed them as living immoral lives. They loved, hated, killed, and warred as they pleased. When the Israelites arrived in the area under the leadership of the prophet Moses, the Canaanite gods were declared "false gods." Baal worshipers were repeatedly persecuted by the Hebrew kings and prophets.

tablets recording the myths of Baal. They also found a stela (an ancient stone slab bearing an inscription or carving) from the second millennium BCE engraved with a picture of Baal. The discoveries gave significant insight into the myths surrounding Baal, his importance, and the way in which he was worshiped.

The Canaanites and Phoenicians

Historians believe that the Canaanites were neither a nation nor an empire, but a collection of different peoples living in villages and towns who shared a common language and followed similar religious beliefs. During the 13th and 12th centuries BCE, much of the territory inhabited by the Canaanites was conquered at various times by the Israelites and the Sea Peoples, invading armies of uncertain origin. Because of the invasions the Canaanites were forced to move to several cities, towns, and small villages along the Mediterranean coast in what is now modern Lebanon.

Over time the Canaanites, it is believed, gave rise to the Phoenicians, and the Phoenicians turned from toiling the land to exploring the Mediterranean. They became great sailors, navigators, and traders. They came in contact with many other Mediterranean peoples, including the Greeks, who developed an alphabet from the Phoenician or Canaanite alphabet of 22 letters. All Western alphabets are based on the Greek-Phoenician alphabet. At the same time, the Phoenician alphabet was adopted by Aramaic peoples and developed into Hebrew and Arabic script, making the Phoenicians the originators of alphabetic writing in the Western and much of the Eastern world.

Mythic Baal

In the myths of Baal the deity was given several titles, including Rider on the Clouds, Thunderer, Master of the Earth, and Strong One. These revealed the superiority of Baal as the storm god. The stela from Ugarit depicts Baal as a young man standing above two wavy lines that may represent either clouds, mountains, or water. In the carving Baal's right hand is raised above his head and he holds a club or mace, perhaps representing thunder. In his left hand he grips a spear, the upper part of which looks like either lightning or a tree. The spear pierces the ground, suggesting that the storm god brings fertility to the earth through rain symbolized by lightning and thunder. The stela may have been intended to represent a scene from one of the myths in which Baal used two clubs—lightning and thunder—to defeat Yam, god of the sea.

In ancient Canaanite mythology Baal lived on Mount Saphon, a high mountain located north of Ugarit. The mountain was well suited as Baal's home because it received the heaviest annual rainfall in the region. Baal was mentioned far more often than his father, Dagon. Baal was also called the "son" of El, head of all the gods. This may mean that Dagon was his father and El was considered his grandfather. Baal may have had several consorts or mates. In Ugaritic mythology, Anat was his main consort, but in the Bible it was often Astarte. Also, Asherah, also spelled Ashtoreth (who is El's consort in the Ugaritic myths), was paired with Baal in the Bible. Anat is also described as his sister in some accounts. The differences may be due to slight variations in belief and practice in the different Canaanite villages and cities.

Baal in conflict with Yam

Three main myths exist about Baal. The first was centered on a conflict between Baal and the goddess Yam. The conflict arose out of the desire of each for total control and possession of the earth. The Canaanites used the conflict of Baal and Yam to explain a natural occurrence. Every year in most of Canaan, toward the end of October, the long, dry summer gave way to a cool, rainy season. The first rains of the season were torrential, and flooding was common. To

Discoveries at Ugarit

Much has been learned about the Canaanite religion from the chance discovery of ancient Ugarit (in modern Syria). Ugarit was a thriving city-state during the second millennia BCE. It was destroyed about 1200 BCE by invaders known as the Sea Peoples, whose origin is uncertain. In the 1920s a Syrian peasant farmer plowing fields near the modern port of Ras Shamra struck a stone that was the shape of a tombstone. He reported the find to the archaeological authorities, who determined that the stone lay in the ancient city of Ugarit. The whole site was excavated in the late 1920s and early 1930s. At one end of the ancient city, the excavators discovered two temples, one to Baal and one to El. Between the two temples there was a building that contained hundreds of clay tablets, some of which have produced glimpses into the mythology of the Canaanites.

Below: This stela from Ugarit was carved around 1900 BCE. It depicts the storm god Baal.

Baal in the Bible

The word *Baal* is ancient Semite or Hebrew for "lord" or "owner" and can be applied to both men and gods. It is still used as a term for a father or husband who is the *baal* (owner) of, for instance, a house, a field, or livestock. According to some biblical scholars, a *baal* was also a local deity who fertilized a district by providing springs for crop irrigation and in return was seen as the owner of the district. The plural of *baal* is *baalim*, and in the Old Testament there are many references to baalim of local places, implying that each village or town had its own baal or deity, such as the Baal of Tyre, the Baal of Tarsus, and the Baal of Lebanon. Baal worship was introduced to the ancient Jews by Jezebel, a queen of Israel. However, the worship of Baal over Yahweh (God) caused major disruption and eventually the Baal worshipers were slaughtered.

According to the Bible, various kinds of animal sacrifices offered with prayers formed part of the rituals connected with Baal worship. Some scholars believe that both sacred prostitution and human sacrifice were also practiced. It seems that these were a form of imitative magic that encouraged the fertility of the land. Participants also cut themselves with knives and lancets to produce a blood offering.

the ancient Canaanites it appeared that Yam was gaining control over the land during the floods. However, Baal had the power to gain control over the waters by conquering her. To have Baal as lord of the earth meant that there would be order and consistency in the rains, and fertility instead of uncontrolled flooding.

In one version of the myth Yam sought to become the sovereign of the earth by defeating Baal in battle. Yam sent two messengers to the assembly of the gods, demanding that they give up Baal. The assembled gods lowered their heads in fear. Baal rebuked them for their cowardice, saying, "I'll answer the messengers of Yam." Then Baal openly confronted her in battle. Taking two clubs made by Kothar, the god of crafts, Baal struck Yam between the eyes, killing her. Having conquered the sea, Baal then became lord of the earth.

Baal, the bringer of rain

In another myth, Baal, as lord of the earth, received permission from El to build a grand palace from which he would reign over the earth. Baal employed Kothar to build his palace. A special window was placed in one of the walls of the palace, through which the rains would flow to water the earth and irrigate all the crops. At the end of the story Baal exclaimed: "I alone will rule over the gods; I alone will fatten gods and men; I alone will satisfy earth's masses." This myth establishes Baal in his role as a god of plenty and fertility—both fertility of the soil and sexual fertility.

Baal goes to the underworld

In a sequel to the myth, Baal's rain began to oversaturate the earth, and the crops were not able to ripen. To stop the rain Baal had to be subdued for a season by Mot, the god of the underworld and drought. Having listened to Baal's

Above: In Carthage, Tunisia, the local deity was named Baal-Hammon. This gravestone depicts his consort, Tanit. The stone marked the grave of human sacrifices to Baal, in about the second or first century BCE.

Right: *This stone altar to the god Baal is found in Baalbek, Lebanon, an important Phoenician town.*

declaration of triumph over all the gods, Mot decided to challenge Baal. He dared Baal to visit the underworld. Baal refused at first, but as champion of the gods he later grew overconfident and descended to the underworld. As he did, he took with him the clouds, the winds, and the rains, but for all his powers, not even Baal could overcome death when he entered the underworld. The rains stopped and the crops were able to mature.

When El heard of Baal's death, he left his throne and sat on the ground. In a state of mourning, he poured dust on his head and covered himself with sackcloth. He then began to cut himself all over with a knife. Anat, Baal's consort in this version of the myth, found Baal's corpse and buried it on Mount Saphon. After mutilating herself, Anat then offered several sacrifices.

Baal's restoration

Finally, El had a vivid dream that made him realize that Baal was not really dead but only held captive in the underworld by Mot. He told Anat about his dream, and in a rage she descended into the underworld and seized Mot. According to the myth, Anat first split Mot with a sword, then winnowed him with a sieve, burned him, and ground him with a mill. She then scattered him over the fields. After Anat's victory the defeated Mot released Baal from the underworld. As a result, fertility returned to the land.

The cycle of Baal conquering Yam, living in his specially built palace and watering the world, descending to the underworld, and being released to bring fresh rain again helped the Canaanites and Phoenicians explain the change of the seasons. The ancient Egyptians had a similar myth involving Isis, Osiris, and Seth. When Seth killed Osiris, Isis reassembled the body, which was resurrected, bringing fertility to the droughted land.

Evidence of worship

From the writings found at Ugarit, as well as from the Bible and other ancient sources, scholars have pieced together some details about the worship of Baal. He, often along with Anat, was worshiped either in temples or in smaller structures often found on hills known as high places. Images of Baal and Anat were placed in the holiest part of the building. An incense altar for prayer was located within the structure, and an altar of sacrifice was in the center of the courtyard. When describing the destruction of Baal worship, some versions of the Bible also refer to the destruction of "groves." In other versions this has been translated as *Ashera* or *Ashtoreth*, which indicates that the groves were places sacred to Baal's consort (see box, page 212). Anat was also considered to be a goddess of fertility and was often represented with a stylized tree beside her.

BRUCE SATTERFIELD

Bibliography

Markoe, Glenn E. *Phoenicians: Peoples of the Past.* Berkeley, CA: University of California Press, 2000.

Nakhai, Beth Alpert. *Archaeology and the Religions of Canaan and Israel.* Atlanta, GA: American Schools of Oriental Research, 2001.

SEE ALSO: Astarte; Canaan and Phoenicia; Flood Myths; Isis; Natural Forces; Osiris; Sacrifice; Seth.

BACCHUS

Originally Bacchus was an alternative name in ancient Greece for Dionysus, the god of wine. Later the Romans used Bacchus as their own god of wine and revelry, but he was a combination of the Greek Dionysus and an ancient Italian wine god named Liber. In Rome the worship of Bacchus formed the center of a dangerous underground cult that was brutally suppressed in the second century BCE.

The son of Jupiter and Semele, the Roman deity Bacchus was god of wine and ecstasy. It was believed he released people from the worries of daily life and brought a sense of personal freedom and happiness. However, there was always an element of danger in the freedom and debauchery associated with Bacchus. If people lost their inhibitions at the expense of their ability to reason, there was no telling what they might do. One example is the story of Pentheus, king of Thebes, and his mother, Agave, known from the ancient drama *Bacchants* (or *Bacchae*) by Euripides (c. 484–406 BCE). Agave (or Agaue), under the influence of Bacchus, was roaming in the mountains when she thought she saw a lion. In a frenzy she killed the beast. When she finally came to her senses, she discovered that she had in fact killed her own son, Pentheus.

Bacchus was usually depicted wearing a wreath of ivy, or occasionally grape vines, around his head. Among his other attributes were wine cups and animal skins, particularly fawn and panther. Sometimes he carried a large wand called a thyrsus, which was a fennel stalk or staff with ivy wound around the top. He often traveled in the company of satyrs and bacchants (or maenads), who were his followers. Satyrs were mythological creatures that usually

Left: This statue titled Bacchus *by Michelangelo was sculpted when the artist was 21 years old. It became the model for later representations.*

had the waist and legs of a goat and the arms and upper body of a man. Bacchants were women who participated in Dionysian rites and revelry. Together the satyrs and bacchants represented the unrestrained forces of nature. Sometimes the god Pan was also included in their company, although he was originally not connected to Bacchus.

Above: *A sixth-century BCE pottery painting by Exekias shows the god of wine making vines spring from his boat's mast while sailing.*

Roman worship

In the official state religion of the Romans, Bacchus played only a minor role (unlike that of Dionysus in Greece), so important sanctuaries of Bacchus were few. There were, however, secret rituals known as Bacchanalia that were especially popular in the south of Italy and were originally held only for women.

The Bacchanalia, or Bacchic Mysteries, were Greek in origin, descended from seasonal festivals called Dionysia. At the core of the Roman Bacchanalia were secret rituals celebrated in private. The exact nature of the rituals are not known because the initiates were sworn to secrecy, but it was popularly believed that sexual orgies were included. What is known, however, is that the ritual included the drinking of wine and that it held out the promise of a happy afterlife to anyone who participated.

In 186 BCE a scandal concerning the Bacchanalia unexpectedly led to the suppression of the cult in Rome (see box, right). The Bacchic cult centers were closed down, with the exception of some venerable ancient shrines. Thousands of worshipers were persecuted. Many fled to the countryside; those who stayed behind were put to death. For more than a century the followers of Bacchus had to hold their meetings in secret, outside the city of Rome. It was not until the time of Julius Caesar (100–44 BCE) that the private worship of Bacchus was officially authorized again.

Representations of Bacchus

In Greek art the god of wine was usually portrayed as a bearded man, although he sometimes appeared beardless. In Roman art Bacchus was more commonly portrayed as a clean-shaven young man. In later art, from the Renaissance

Scandalous Bacchanalia

In 186 BCE there was a great scandal in Rome concerning the Bacchanalia. A young nobleman named Publius Aebutius almost became the victim of a violent type of Bacchic cult. After the death of his father, his mother had remarried an immoral man who squandered almost the entire estate of his stepson, who was still underage. The mother and stepfather then decided to get rid of Aebutius by having him initiated into a dangerous Bacchic cult. Tradition has it that the young man was saved by his girlfriend, Hispala, who had accompanied Aebutius's mother to this particular cult on earlier occasions. She had seen things there that had terrified her, and she warned Aebutius that he would suffer an unspeakable fate, perhaps even death, if he joined the group. Aebutius went to the authorities with Hispala, who gave key evidence about the nature of the Bacchanalia. The matter was brought before the Senate, which immediately passed a law prohibiting the Bacchanalia.

Bacchus in Pompeii

In 79 CE Mount Vesuvius erupted, covering the neighboring town of Pompeii under a thick layer of volcanic ash. Because the ash layer was airtight, many objects and wall paintings were preserved until excavation work began in the mid-18th century.

In the House of the Centenary (so called because it was excavated in 1879, eighteen hundred years after the eruption), a wall painting (below) shows a landscape with Bacchus standing at the foot of Vesuvius as the volcano may have looked before the eruption. In the painting, the lower part of the mountain is covered with vineyards, and Bacchus is depicted as a giant bunch of grapes with human arms, head, and feet. With his right hand he pours wine to a panther; in his left hand he holds a thyrsus.

In the Villa of the Mysteries, built between 70 and 60 BCE, there is a room decorated on three walls with scenes relating to the Mysteries of Bacchus. The exact meaning of the scenes remains unclear. The central scene on the back wall shows the god himself lying in the arms of Ariadne. To the right a kneeling woman is about to uncover a secret object hidden in a winnowing basket.

Below: Bacchus and Mount Vesuvius, *a fresco painting from the House of the Centenary, Pompeii. The depiction of the god of wine as a bunch of grapes is rare but clearly shows who the subject is.*

Above: *This 19th-century painting, titled* Bacchanal, *by Lawrence Alma-Tadema (1836–1912), is the artist's impression of a Roman bacchanal, or drinking party.*

(15th and 16th centuries) onward, he was often depicted as a fat drunkard, the personification of excess.

In sculpture perhaps the most influential piece is Michelangelo's statue *Bacchus* (1496–1497), where the deity appears as a drunken adolescent. The depiction and pose of Michelangelo's Bacchus served as an example to many later sculptors of the character. In painting, Bacchus was often accompanied by a merry group of satyrs and bacchants. Many times he was paired with Ariadne, whom he consoled after she was abandoned by Theseus. The motif of the bacchanal (drinking party) was also common. Titian (c. 1489–1576) was the Renaissance standard-bearer of

mythological art, and he created the prototype for Bacchus and many other Greek and Roman mythological characters. Titian's *Bacchanal* and *Bacchus and Ariadne* (both 1522–1523) are two famous examples that were models for later painters of mythological scenes, such as Peter Paul Rubens (1577–1640) and Nicolas Poussin (1594–1665).

Bacchus and Christianity

In Christian art and literature Bacchus was sometimes regarded as a prefiguration (early form) of Christ. Like Christ, Bacchus was the son of a god and a mortal woman and extended the promise of a blissful afterlife. A floor mosaic in Cyprus shows a scene that looks similar to the familiar scene of the Virgin Mary holding the young Jesus, commonly referred to as the Madonna and Child. Instead of the Madonna in the mosaic there is Hermes (Mercury in Rome), who, according to legend, took the infant deity to be raised by bacchants. The infant Bacchus is depicted, like Jesus, with a halo around his head.

Early Christian art also made ample use of Bacchic symbolism, attaching new meaning to old symbols. The grapevines that had for centuries decorated Roman tombs as a symbol of everlasting life came to be used as a symbol for the Christian afterlife. An early example of this is found in the Santa Constanza in Rome, which was built between 337 and 361 as a mausoleum for Constantia, the daughter of Rome's first Christian emperor, Constantine the Great (who ruled 306–337). One of the ceiling mosaics in the mausoleum shows a large portrait of Constantia surrounded by swirling vines and men harvesting grapes, and her sarcophagus is decorated with cupids harvesting grapes.

FEYO SCHUDDEBOOM

Bibliography

Bulfinch, Thomas. *Bulfinch's Mythology.* New York: Modern Library, 1998.

Euripides, and Paul Roche, trans. *10 Plays*. New York: Signet Classic, 1998.

Fleming, Stuart. *Vinum: The Story of Roman Wine*. Glen Mills, PA: Art Flair, 2001.

Howatson, M. C., and Ian Chilvers. *Concise Oxford Companion to Classical Literature.* New York: Oxford University Press, 1993.

SEE ALSO: Ariadne; Dionysus; Faunus; Festivals; Pan; Rome; Satyrs.

BALDER

In Norse mythology Balder was a beautiful god of light, famous for his purity and kindness. However, he was most significant for the ancient Scandinavians because of the story of his death, which was engineered by the cunning tricks of the god Loki.

The ancient Scandinavians were a fierce, warrior-like people who worshiped gods that were also warriors. Yet one deity was an exception—Balder, whom they admired because of his kindness and good nature. According to both the *Poetic Edda* and the 13th-century Icelander Snorri Sturluson's *Prose Edda*, Balder had a high social position among the deities because he was the son of Odin, king of the gods, and Frigga, goddess of love. He was also the most popular god of Asgard, the celestial dwelling place of the gods. The only god who resented Balder's popularity was Loki, the devilish trickster. In contrast to Balder, the cruel and deceitful Loki was treated as an outcast among the Asgard gods. The Scandinavians also believed that Loki was the cause of earthquakes and volcanic eruptions, which are still common in Iceland.

Death and protection

When Balder began to have nightmares and premonitions about dying, all the gods, except Loki, grew worried. Odin rode his eight-legged horse, Sleipnir, to Niflheim, the underworld, where he tricked a soothsayer into telling him that Balder's blind twin brother, Höd, would be the agent of Balder's death. Odin doubted the revelation because there was no animosity between Höd and Balder. Meanwhile, Frigga (or her maids) traveled through all nine worlds of the Norse mythological universe, persuading every living thing not to harm Balder. However, she did not bother to get a promise from the mistletoe, assuming that such an innocent plant could never harm her son.

Soon after Frigga's return to Asgard, an entertainment was planned. Knowing that nothing could harm him, Balder agreed to be a target against which the others could test their weapons. When swords and spears fell away from Balder, he and all the gods laughed. Hearing their merriment, Loki grew jealous; he vowed to destroy Balder.

Right: This mid-19th century statue of Balder reflects its description as "Balder the glorious." Balder was considered to be responsible for the rising of the sun and long summer days.

Loki's revenge

Loki transformed himself into an old woman and entered Frigga's hall, where he gained Frigga's confidence by getting the goddess to talk of all the good things her

Left: A manuscript illustrating the Poetic Edda, *a series of poems about the Norse gods, shows the death of Balder (right) at the hand of his twin brother Höd. Manipulative Loki guides the shaft. This manuscript was produced in the 16th century by an Icelandic priest. It can be seen at the Royal Library in Copenhagen, Denmark.*

son had done. Then Loki maneuvered the conversation onto the subject of Balder's premonitions and asked Frigga if she had really made every living thing promise not to hurt her son. Frigga admitted that she had overlooked the mistletoe. Loki hurried off to find some mistletoe, from which he made a deadly dart. When Loki returned to the entertainment, the dart was hidden under his cloak.

Loki convinced Höd to participate in the game of trying to wound Balder by promising that he would make up for Höd's blindness by guiding the throw. Loki placed the mistletoe dart in Höd's hand and pointed it at Balder. Höd's throw with Loki's aim proved fatal for Balder. The gentle god fell to the ground. As the other gods hovered around him, wringing their hands, he died.

When Höd learned what he had done, he cried out in grief, shoving Loki away from him. The gods then understood the full horror of Loki's treachery and chased him away with threats and curses. (In a Danish version of the myth, Balder and Höd were rivals for Nanna, who became Balder's wife, and Höd killed Balder out of jealousy.) Heartbroken over Balder's death, they decorated a longship with flowers and thorns, which were emblems of sleep, then set the ship afire. All Balder's favorite possessions were put on the ship with him, even his horse. Balder's floating funeral pyre drifted out to sea as the gods wept and watched the flames consume him.

Balder in the underworld

Overcome with longing for her beloved son, Frigga offered herself as a prize to any god who would go to the underworld and bring Balder back. Hermód, another brother of Balder's, took up the challenge. Riding on Sleipnir, Hermód traveled to the land of the dead. During his nine-day journey through the misty hills and dark valleys of the underworld, Hermód learned that Balder had journeyed into the depths of Niflheim accompanied by 500 warriors on horseback. (In another version Höd was sent to Hel with Balder as punishment for causing his death.)

Balder and Christ

Norse gods were usually grim, aggressive warriors, reflecting the Scandinavians' violent existence, but the kind Balder was the exception. The story of Balder shows that the Norse also had a place for kindness and generosity. It is also possible that Balder formed a link between pagan and Christian Scandinavia. Both Balder and Jesus were solar deities, associated with light—Balder emanated light because of his beauty and goodness, and Jesus was meant to shine the metaphorical light of Christianity onto a dark and lost world. Both were also innocents who suffered an unjust death. Balder, however, was not resurrected like Jesus. In fact, Balder's death brought the destruction of everything. Nevertheless, the two figures must have been linked in the minds of some Norse: a stone pillar was discovered bearing carvings of both Balder's and Jesus' death.

Right: *After their conversion to Christianity around 1,000 years ago, the Vikings used the skills that they had developed through boat building to construct pagoda-like temples, known as stave churches, such as this one here. Some examples that are over 800 years old are still standing.*

Hermód called on Hel, goddess of the underworld, and begged her to return Balder to the land of the living. Hel took pity on Hermód. She promised to let Balder go if every creature mourned the dead god—but if even one did not, Balder would be hers forever.

Meanwhile, the gods drove Loki from Asgard. As he was being forced out, he shouted that by killing Balder he had engineered the coming of Ragnarok, the predestined destruction of Asgard, the gods, and all living things. He then transformed himself into a giantess named Thokk and sat in a mountain cave, hidden from the gods. Soon afterward messengers were sent to ask all living things to weep for the dead Balder. The gods had high hopes that their attempt would be successful and that Balder would return in triumph. Then a messenger entered Thokk's cave, and the giant refused to weep. The messenger returned to Asgard in despair. He reported that out of the whole world one lone being would not weep for Balder. Loki had won: Balder remained in Niflheim, and the gods had to prepare for Ragnarok. According to some versions, after Ragnarok Balder and his brother Höd would rise from Hel into the new world.

Comparisons and conversions

Balder seems to have played an important part in the spread of Christianity through Scandinavia. The conversion of Scandinavia began in the eighth century and lasted until roughly the 13th century. Christianity first arrived in Scandinavia when Vikings, while raiding abroad, abducted Christians and forced them into slavery. Gradually Christian

Above: The glowing longship carrying the body of Balder is launched into the turbulent sea in this 1893 painting by Frank Dicksee (1853–1928).

missionaries spread through northern Europe, although many monasteries were raided by Vikings. Around 960, Denmark's King Harald Bluetooth officially adopted Christianity for his whole kingdom. In 1024 King Olaf (later Saint Olaf) formally began the Christian church in Norway, ending more than a decade of active conversion, during which he had employed missionaries from England to preach to Norwegians throughout the country. The Swedes' conversion followed in the 13th century, although Sweden's own King Olaf tried but failed to impose Christianity on his country during his reign, which lasted from 995 to 1022.

During Scandinavia's transition from pagan beliefs to Christianity, Balder was probably compared to Jesus Christ, and some scholars speculate that the comparison made the acceptance of Christ and other Biblical characters easier. Perhaps for many Norsemen the Biblical Jesus was Balder returned from the dead, bringing with him a new heaven and a new earth.

Another common comparison between a Norse deity and a Biblical character involves Loki, whose part in the ruin of Asgard corresponds to the role of Satan in Eden. Comparisons have also been made between Balder and mythological characters from other cultures. He has similar characteristics to Apollo, the Greek sun god, who also had a twin brother. Osiris in Egypt and Tammuz in Mesopotamia were also beloved solar deities who died young and sank into the underworld.

Some scholars have suggested that in the cold, long winters of Scandinavia, the figure of Balder might well have inspired an even greater devotion among his followers than did similar deities in the warm Mediterranean cultures.

BARBARA GARDNER

Bibliography

Larrington, Carolyne, trans. *The Poetic Edda.* New York: Oxford University Press, 1996.

Snorri Sturluson and Anthony Faulkes, trans. *Edda.* New York: Oxford University Press, 1991.

SEE ALSO: Aesir; Apocalypse Myths; Frigga; Hel; Hermód; Líf and Leifthrasir; Loki; Odin; Scandinavia.

BALTIC, THE

The ancestors of the modern Estonians, Latvians, and Lithuanians were known as the Balts. Elements of their nature-based mythology can still be found in some Baltic rituals today.

The Balts lived along the southeastern edge of the Baltic Sea, which forms part of the Atlantic Ocean and is located to the east of Scandinavia and the north of present-day Poland. Like all ancient peoples, the Balts understood their world according to natural phenomena and agricultural cycles. By taking note of astronomical events, such as phases of the moon, seasonal sunrise and sunset patterns, and solstices and equinoxes, they were able to schedule agricultural work and annual religious festivals and ceremonies. The Balts worshiped a number of gods, and many of the Baltic deities were personifications of natural phenomena. The chief deity was Dievas, who was also called Praamzius, Satvaras, or Prakurimas, depending on the region. The name Dievas is Indo-European in origin and is related to those of the Indo-Aryan god Dyaus and the Greek god Zeus. The word is also similar to the Latin word *deus*, which means "god."

The Balts perceived the sun as a goddess named Saule and the moon as the god Menulis. The planets were believed to be Saule's daughters, collectively known as the Saules meitas. Saule's eldest daughter was Zeme, an earth goddess. Among her other daughters were Ausrine and Vakarine, who personified two aspects of the planet Venus—Ausrine

Above: *Both the sun and the Baltic Sea featured in many sacred myths of the ancient Balts. It was believed that Saule, the sun goddess, lived above the Baltic Sea and drove a chariot of fire across the daytime sky.*

appeared in the morning, while Vakarine appeared in the evening. Saule's daughter Indraja was identified with the planet Jupiter, Selija was Saturn, Ziezdre was Mars, and Vaivora was believed to be Mercury. In Latvia, meanwhile, Auseklis was the name of Morning Venus, while Rieteklis was Evening Venus.

Seasonal festivals

The Balts marked the change of seasons by performing ceremonies and holding festivals. In winter they celebrated the solstice with a ritual to honor Dievas. This was the most important ceremony of the Baltic calendar, and it lasted for 12 days. During the festival homage was paid to the souls of ancestors. After the winter solstice festival the Balts celebrated Pusiauziemis, usually on January 25. At the beginning of February a set of days was dedicated to the awakening of household gods.

The spring holiday of Jurgines was held on April 23. Eggs were hardboiled, painted, and colored, then given to children. Adults celebrated by cooking scrambled eggs, feasting, singing, and dancing. During the festival sacred trees were carefully planted so as not to break any green branches.

Summer had one major festival, the Svente of Rasa. Rasa was the goddess of the morning dew, and the festival dedicated to her was celebrated near the end of June on or near the summer solstice. Today the people of the Baltic celebrate a similar festival known by its Christian name, Saint John's Day.

The Velines were observed at the end of October or beginning of November. These were holy days in remembrance of the Veles, or "Shades," during which it was believed that the dead would gather and feast alongside the living. Also a harvest ritual was performed in honor of cereal deities, such as the Rugiu Boba (rye-wives). During the ceremony, idols made of the last sheaf of rye were carried in a procession.

Religious beliefs and sacrifices

The Balts often held rituals near sacred streams because they believed that deities, mermaids, spirits, and souls of drowned humans lived in the water. This belief led to a respect for water that stopped the people from polluting the streams. The Balts also built temples, and the remains of some dating from the third and fourth centuries CE have been discovered on mounds near the Sozh River in modern Belarus. Archaeologists have also uncovered Baltic temples dating from the fifth to sixth centuries on Blagoveshchensk Hill near Briansk, and others dating from the first to fifth centuries on the Backininkeliai Mound near Prienai. Other ancient sites include the Romove Temple in Prussia, the Perkunas Temple in Vilnius (dedicated to the god of thunder), and the Milda Temple near Kaunas, sacred to the goddess of love.

The Tale of the Castle of Vilnius

One Lithuanian folktale tells how a duke named Gediminas offered a sacrifice to the gods to make his castle impregnable. Gediminas built the castle on the highest hill so that no army could attack it. A huge rock was chosen as the cornerstone. Priests gathered for the stone-setting ceremony and were asked to decide on a suitable sacrifice. They determined a mother must willingly offer her firstborn son. One old woman brought forward her only son, who was a young man. The son did not question his mother's decision, but challenged the priests' divination with three riddles, asking: "Oh Wise Ones, tell me what in all of creation is the sweetest, the lightest, and the hardest?" The priests answered: "The sweetest substance in the world is the honeycomb of the wild bees. The lightest thing in the world is the down of wild birds. The hardest is the sword of our grand duke, which can strike an armored knight in half!"

"No!" said the young man. "For the babe, his mother's milk is sweeter. For the mother, nothing is lighter than the child in her arms. And nothing is harder than my mother's heart, if without it breaking, she can offer her only son to such a fate."

The grand duke agreed with the young man, who was freed. The priests again asked the gods to reveal a fitting offering: They chose the fairest, most virtuous maiden, lovely as a wildflower, with sky blue eyes and a shining purity of spirit. She was placed in the foundation ditch, where she stood in white bridal robes with a bouquet of flowers in her hands.

The crowd hushed, and the cornerstone was pushed into the ditch. Gediminas looked down into the ditch. Suddenly he exclaimed: "The gods themselves have chosen the sacrifice most favorable in their eyes!" Everyone rushed to see. Below stood the maiden, alive and well. On her cheeks glittered two large diamonds—tears for the flowers knocked from her hands and crushed by the heavy rock. As a result of the maiden's sacrifice the castle of Vilnius was the strongest in the land. The grand duke married the fair maiden, and the wise youth became the grand duke's adviser.

***Above:** This lakeside Latvian farmhouse is typical of rural dwellings in the Baltic. The ancient Balts believed that lakes such as this were home to a variety of spirits and water deities.*

Archaeologists have also uncovered evidence suggesting that the Lithuanian Balts may have practiced human sacrifice. Most of the remains have been dated to between 100 BCE and 500 CE, but some, including fractured skull fragments, date from much earlier. Another find, from a graveyard in Duonkalnis, was of a young man believed to be a priest or oracle because he was buried with sacred objects such as amulets made from animal teeth. Placed crookedly at his feet were the remains of a woman who may have been sacrificed. Some scholars argue that many of the finds were not the remains of people who had been ritually sacrificed, but were those of people who had died due to other violent causes such as war or murder. If, however, the Balts did practice human sacrifice, the tale of the Castle of Vilnius may hold the clue as to why the practice stopped (see box, left).

Religious leaders acted as advisers to rulers. There were three different types of religious leaders: *kriviai* (priests), *zyniai* (sorcerers-magicians-diviners-sages), and *vaidilos* (bardic priests). As in the tale of the Castle of Vilnius, people could question the priests' interpretations of divine will and challenge the priests with three riddles—riddles were an integral part of Baltic lore.

The Baltic Sea

The Baltic Sea played an important role in the mythology of the region. One myth tells of the death of the beautiful mermaid-goddess Jurate, who lived in an amber palace in the Baltic Sea. Kastytis, a fisherman, would often cast his nets to catch fish from Jurate's realm. One day the goddess sent her mermaids to warn the man to stop fishing in her

Major Baltic Gods and Goddesses

The following are some of the major deities of the ancient Baltic pantheon.

Ausautas:	God of health; similar to the Greek god Asclepius.
Ausrine:	Also Auseklis, goddess of the dawn; represented as the planet Venus or Morning Venus.
Dekla:	Goddess of fortune and destiny.
Dievas:	Also known as Praamzius, Prakurimas, and Satvaras, ruler of time, creator god, and supreme deity of the Baltic pantheon.
Dimste:	A household goddess.
Jurate:	Mermaid-goddess of the Baltic Sea.
Kaupole:	Goddess of vegetation.
Laukamate:	Goddess of fields and fertility.
Mara:	Goddess of fate and one of the holy trinity in the Dievturiba revivalist religion.
Menulis:	Protector of travelers and soldiers, source of light at night, and father of Zemes; represented as the moon.
Mezamate:	Also known as Mother of the Forest, goddess of the forest and all creatures.
Milda:	Goddess of love and freedom.
Nijole:	A goddess of the underworld.
Nonadieve:	A household goddess.
Perkunas:	Also called Percunis or Perkons, god of thunder.
Pikuolis:	Also called Pykuolis, god of the dead and the underworld.
Patrimpas:	God of harvests.
Ragana:	A seeress or witch who revealed the future and controlled supernatural powers.
Rasa:	Goddess of morning dew.
Saule:	Most powerful of heavenly goddesses and mother of Zemes; represented as the sun.
Saules meitas:	Daughters of Saule.
Usins:	Latvian god of light and horses.
Vejamate:	Also called Veju Motina, Mother of the Winds and the guardian of the woods and birds.
Velnias:	A god of the underworld.
Zeme:	Also known as Zemes mate, Mother of the Soil; goddess of welfare and fertile fields, eldest daughter of Saule (sun) and Menulis (moon); represented as the earth.
Zaltys:	A sacred serpent.

domain, but he refused. Jurate went to speak to the man herself; when she saw how handsome and courageous Kastytis was, she fell in love with him and brought him to her palace. Dievas, angered by the love affair, ordered the thunder god Perkunas to kill Jurate.

The Baltic Sea also played an important part in myths about Saule, the beautiful sun goddess who lived across the Baltic Sea. (The only other female sun goddess in world mythology is the Japanese goddess Amaterasu.) Every morning Saule drove a brilliant chariot of gold, copper, or fire pulled by two white horses into the sky. In the evening she changed the chariot into a golden boat that was steered across the Baltic Sea by the goddess Perkunele, who bathed the tired and dusty Saule and saw her off each morning, refreshed and shining for a new day's journey. Other myths recounted that one goddess, Vakarine, made the bed for Saule, and another goddess, Ausrine, stoked the fire for Saule and made her ready for another day's journey. By all accounts, Ausrine was a maiden of remarkable beauty. She wore a starry mantle with a moon-shaped brooch on her shoulder, had golden hair, and had an image of Saule on her crown.

Saule and Menulis

Saule's husband was Menulis, a young god dressed in silver who was the guardian of night and time. Menulis and Saule featured in a myth that explained solar eclipses. The two deities covered themselves with a wrap so that their daughter, Zeme, the earth deity, would not see them kissing.

Above: A solar eclipse. The ancient Balts explained eclipses through the myth of Saule and Menulis.

Above: *This illustration is based on a woodcut of ancient Lithuanians worshiping the sun goddess Saule.*

In other myths, Saule and Menulis were divorced, which explained why the sun and the moon never rose or set together. In one story, the moon married the sun in the primeval spring. Because the sun rose early, the moon separated and walked alone. He met Ausrine and fell in love with her. Perkunas punished the moon by striking him with his sword, causing his face to appear cut in half. The rift between the sun and the moon was also explained in a Latvian myth. The moon kidnapped the bridegroom Auseklis (the Latvian name for Morning Venus). The sun accused the moon of the crime, and the two heavenly bodies never forgave each other.

One of the major gods of Baltic mythology was known as Perkunas or Perkons. He was associated with rain, thunder, and lightning, and was usually depicted holding a sword, an iron rod, a golden whip, a fiery club, or a knife. Perkunas also used his arms to create thunder and lightning. Historians believe that the small axes on the clothing of the ancient Balts were most likely worn in honor of Perkunas.

Surviving traditions

By the 14th century most Balts had been converted to Christianity. Latvia was converted in the 13th century by German Livonian knights, and Lithuania, the last pagan country in Europe, became Christian in the 14th century. However, elements of pagan beliefs survived as folklore, ballads, and songs. Some rituals continue, such as a wedding tradition in which the bride bids goodbye to her paternal home by praying and making sacrifices to a straw representation of Nonadieve, a household goddess. Another traditional custom that survives occurs when the new crescent moon appears. People address it as Dievaitis (Young God) and pray for good health. Although their original ritualistic significance is lost, Lithuanian names for day (*diena*), night (*naktis*), day and night (*para*), and specific hours of day and night are still used today.

In 1925 a revivalist religion called Dievturiba ("Having God") was established in Latvia by Ernests Brastins (1892–1942). He wanted to strengthen Latvian national identity with a religion based on the Baltic past. It focused on a trinity of deities: Dievs was the heavenly ruler, Mara was the goddess of the material, and Laime (or Laima) was the goddess of destiny. Lithuania saw the establishment of a similar revivalist religion called Romuva. Through these religions, the folklore, poetry, songs, and other ancient mythological traditions of the Baltic region have lived on.

ALYS CAVINESS

Bibliography

Greimas, Algirdas, and Milda Newman, trans. *Of Gods and Men: Studies in Lithuanian Mythology.* Bloomington, IN: Indiana University Press, 1992.

Russell, Charles Coulter, and Patricia Turner. *Encyclopedia of Ancient Deities.* Jefferson, NC: McFarland and Company, 2000.

SEE ALSO: Ancestor Worship; Festivals; Moon; Sacrifice; Sun.

BELLEROPHON

In Greek mythology Bellerophon was a hero who tamed the winged horse Pegasus and slew a fearsome monster known as the Chimera. Bellerophon's story carried him from Greece to Lycia, in what is now Turkey, where he had most of his adventures.

Bellerophon was born in Corinth, which is a city and surrounding area in Greece that was considered sacred to Poseidon, god of the sea. Bellerophon was the son of Glaucus and Eurymede, and the grandson of Sisyphus. One mythological source claims that Poseidon was the real father of Bellerophon, although Glaucus raised him without knowing his true origins. His travels took him to Lycia in what is now southwestern Turkey, and he is credited in legend with introducing Greek culture to that region.

The earliest version of Bellerophon's story is found in the *Iliad*, the great epic poem from the eighth-century BCE by Homer. It tells the story of the Trojan War, and in the sixth book Bellerophon's grandson, the Lycian Glaucus, narrates Bellerophon's story.

Left: This illustration, based on a 17th-century woodcut, shows Bellerophon with the winged horse Pegasus, which he tamed.

Flight to Lycia

For some unexplained reason Bellerophon had to leave Corinth and travel southward through the hills to Argos. One version has it that he fled Corinth because he had accidentally killed his brother. King Proetus (or Proitus) of Argos received him kindly, but the king's wife, Anteia (or Stheneboea), fell in love with the handsome Bellerophon as soon as she saw him. Queen Anteia wanted Bellerophon to become her secret lover. When he rejected her advances, she was furious. The spiteful Anteia lied to Proetus, announcing that Bellerophon had made advances toward her. Proetus felt betrayed and angry but could not bring himself to kill Bellerophon. Instead he sent the young Corinthian across the sea to Lycia, where Anteia's father, Iobates, was king. On arriving in Lycia, Bellerophon was to give Iobates a folded and sealed tablet containing a message for the king. Unknown to Bellerophon, the message instructed Iobates to kill the handsome Corinthian.

When Bellerophon landed in Lycia, Iobates received him with a feast that lasted nine days. On the 10th day he asked Bellerophon for the tablet and read the contents. Although stunned by Proetus' murderous request, Iobates did not want to incur the wrath of the gods by killing an important guest. Instead he sent Bellerophon on a series of dangerous tasks, not expecting him to survive.

Slaying the Chimera

First Bellerophon had to kill the Chimera. The word *chimera* is Greek for "goat," but this was a much more fearsome creature than any ordinary goat. The mythological Chimera was a fire-breathing monster with the head of a lion, a body with a goat's head rising from it, and a snake as a tail. Bellerophon killed the monster. The king then sent him to fight the ferocious Solymi, a neighboring warrior tribe. Legends describe the battle between Bellerophon and the Solymi as the fiercest ever known, with Bellerophon emerging victorious. Bellerophon then had to fight the Amazons, a race of warrior women, but they too failed to kill him.

When Iobates heard that Bellerophon had survived the Amazons, the king sent his own soldiers to ambush him on his way back. Bellerophon killed every one of them. Then the king knew that this was a hero who was part divine, reinforcing the possibility that Poseidon was his real father. He ennobled Bellerophon and allowed him to marry his younger daughter and Anteia's sister, Philonoe. Together the couple had three children, who became the ancestors of the Lycian royal house.

The winged horse

In a parallel version of Bellerophon's adventures, the Corinthian hero was accompanied by Pegasus, the winged horse. Pegasus, according to some, was the child of Medusa and Poseidon, and in Corinth, a favorite site of Poseidon's, there was a large fountain named for the winged horse. One day Bellerophon saw Pegasus drinking water from a well. He leaped onto the winged horse but could not tame it. Then Athena, goddess of war and wisdom, gave Bellerophon a golden bridle. He slipped the bridle on Pegasus and tamed the horse immediately. The Corinthians built a temple called Athena of the Bridle in honor of the story.

Bellerophon remembered

Bellerophon's story is told in writings by Pindar, a lyric poet of the fifth century BCE, and by Pausanias, a second-century CE historian, who described the cities of Greece. Following the marriage to Iobates' daughter, the rest of Bellerophon's myth was told in two works by Euripides

Right: *This terra-cotta relief, dating from 450 BCE, shows Bellerophon slaying the three-headed Chimera. The Chimera was reputed to have the strength of three beasts and to breathe fire. An active volcano in Lycia also had the name Chimera.*

Innocent Heroes and Jealous Older Women

There are many stories in which an older woman tries to seduce an innocent young man and then lies about him. One example is the Biblical character Joseph from the Book of Genesis. Joseph was sold as a slave to an Egyptian named Potiphar, whom he served well. One day when Potiphar was away, his wife tried to seduce Joseph, who ran away. Potiphar's wife then accused Joseph of raping her, and Potiphar had him cast into prison. While there he interpreted the dreams of others and by doing so earned his freedom.

A comparable Greek myth tells of the love of Phaedra for her stepson Hippolytus. When Hippolytus refused Phaedra's advances, the older woman made it seem that Hippolytus had attacked her. The young man's father then cursed him. As a result of the curse, Poseidon caused Hippolytus to be killed by his own horses.

There are also modern versions of the story, such as *The Graduate*. Originally a novel by Charles Webb, *The Graduate* was turned into a popular movie in 1967. The story is about a young college graduate, Benjamin Braddock, who is enticed into an affair by the wife of his father's friend. Benjamin, like the biblical Joseph and Bellerophon, triumphs over the jealous anger and schemes of the older woman.

Above: This fourth-century mosaic found in a building in Nabeul, Tunisia, shows Bellerophon's bride, Philonoe, the daughter of the King of Lycia.

(c. 484–406 BCE), a Greek playwright. Bellerophon, according to Euripides, never forgot Anteia's wrongs against him, and one day he mounted Pegasus and flew back to Argos. There he found Anteia crying because she still loved the hero. Pretending to take pity on her, he invited her to fly with him back to Lycia. She eagerly climbed onto Pegasus and sat behind Bellerophon, but when they were high in the sky far above the sea, he let her fall. This was Bellerophon's revenge on both her and, through Anteia's death, on Proetus. In another version Anteia committed suicide when she heard that her sister had married Bellerophon.

Flying too high

In one of Euripides' other plays, Pegasus played a key role in Bellerophon's most foolish adventure. The hero wanted to see Mount Olympus, the home of the gods. He mounted the winged horse and flew up to the mountain, but as he got closer Zeus caused him to fall off Pegasus. Bellerophon had met a similar fate to other Greek mythological characters who grew too arrogant while flying. For example, Icarus and Phaethon, both fell from the sky. Although Bellerophon did not die from the fall, he was left lame. He landed in a mysterious place called the Plain of Wandering, where, according to legend, he hobbled forever, avoiding human company and consumed with grief. Meanwhile Pegasus went on to Olympus, where the winged horse became steed of the gods.

JAMES M. REDFIELD

Bibliography

Bulfinch, Thomas. *Bulfinch's Mythology.* New York: Modern Library, 1998.

Homer, and Robert Fagles, trans. *The Iliad.* New York: Penguin USA, 2003.

SEE ALSO: Amazons; Animals; Demigods and Heroes; Icarus; Phaethon; Poseidon; Sisyphus; Zeus.

BERGELMIR

According to Old Norse mythology, Bergelmir was the son of the frost giant Thrúdgelmir and the grandson of Ymir, the first frost giant. He and his wife were the only giants to have survived when Odin, father of the gods, killed Ymir, whose blood drowned the world.

The Old Norse creation myth tells that Ymir was nurtured on the milk of the primeval cow Audhumla in the place known as Ginnungagap, a vast mythical void that existed during the time before creation. From one of Ymir's legs grew an ugly six-headed frost giant named Thrúdgelmir (also called Prudgelmir, the Powerful Shouting One). Variations on the creation myth have it that Thrúdgelmir was created from Ymir's sweat. Thrúdgelmir was in turn the father of Bergelmir, but nothing is said in the creation myth about whether Bergelmir was born from a giantess or created in a similar way to Thrúdgelmir.

Conflicting versions of Bergelmir's story

Bergelmir the frost giant is mentioned in both of the major sources for Norse mythology, the *Prose Edda* and *Poetic Edda*. The *Prose Edda* is a mythological text written about 1220 by the Icelandic scholar and historian Snorri Sturluson (1179–1241) and intended for skalds (court poets). The *Poetic Edda* is a collection of mythological and heroic poems, which survives in the Codex Regius (c. 1270), a manuscript now in Reykjavík, Iceland.

Below: The wintry, mountainous landscape of Norway was the dwelling place of mythological frost giants such as Bergelmir.

The *Prose Edda* and the *Poetic Edda* give different versions of the Bergelmir story. The former tells that the chief god, Odin, and his brothers Vili and Vé killed the first frost giant Ymir and used his body parts to create the world. In the flood caused by Ymir's spilled blood, all the frost giants perished, except for Bergelmir and his wife, who escaped together in a *lúdr*. Scholars believe that *lúdr*, a rare word, refers to a hollow wooden device that was either an ark, box, coffin, or cradle. There is disagreement on the exact meaning because the literal translation of the word is "trumpet."

In the *Poetic Edda* the wise giant Vafthrúdnir and Odin engaged in an epic riddle contest. During the match Vafthrúdnir named Thrúdgelmir and Aurgelmir (Ymir) as Bergelmir's father and grandfather. Vafthrúdnir also claimed that the earliest thing he could remember was the birth of Bergelmir, which had happened countless years before the world was made. He could also remember the moment when Bergelmir was placed in a *lúdr*. (In this context *lúdr* could be either "coffin" or "cradle.") The *Poetic Edda* does not mention a flood, and scholars conclude that the alternative version in the *Prose Edda* combines Christian elements with traditional pagan material. Snorri was, after all, a Christian author writing more than 200 years after the conversion of Iceland to Christianity. He seems to have imagined Bergelmir and his wife being saved in the same way as Noah had survived the Great Flood in the book of Genesis in the Old Testament. Bergelmir and his wife became the ancestors of a new generation of frost giants, who were to be the enemies of the gods, especially those of the Aesir, until Ragnarok, the final battle between the gods and the giants.

Below: *A page from the Codex Regius, the oldest manuscript of the* Poetic Edda, *one source of our knowledge of the giant Bergelmir.*

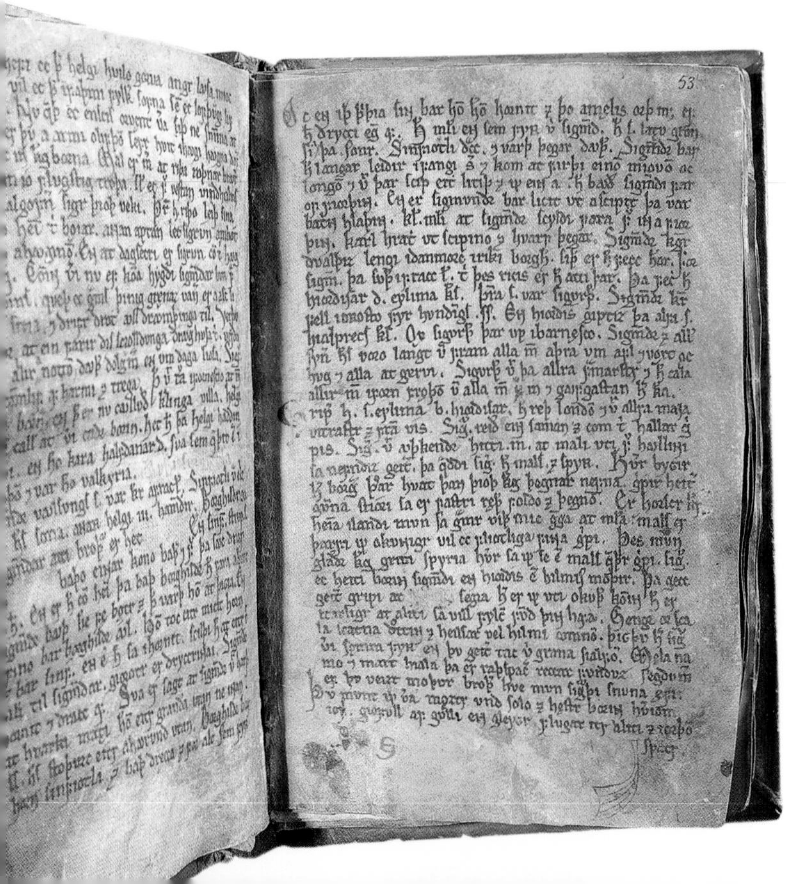

Possible origins of Bergelmir

Bergelmir's name has been translated by scholars of ancient Scandinavian mythology as "mountain bellower." Another translation, however, divides the frost giant's name as "ber-gelmir" rather than "berg-gelmir," suggesting the phrase "the one who roars like a bear" rather than "the one who roars like a mountain." Names of giants often contained an element of roaring or bellowing or a connection with rocks and mountains.

Frost giants, such as Bergelmir, were the most common type of giants in Norse mythology. Others included fire giants and mountain giants, though often they were not entirely distinct. Frost giants were associated with the frozen regions of the mythical North and East, and they were said to inhabit Jötunheim, with its citadel Utgard. Their mead hall, a special meeting place in Norse culture and mythology, was called Ókolnir, which either means "not-cooling," a name probably relating to fire giants rather than to frost giants, or is an error for *Ofkolnir*, which means "extremely cold."

There was no cult connected with Bergelmir, mainly because frost giants were not venerated as divine beings in Old Norse religion. Instead they were considered evil creatures and the enemies of the gods. In this they can be compared to the Titans in Greek mythology. Giants had elements of chaos and destruction and usually were considered to be either extremely stupid (because they were linked to inanimate objects such as mountains or rocks) or extremely wise, but with a wisdom derived from experience due to their antiquity rather than from intellectual capacities.

DONATA KICK

Bibliography:

Larrington, Carolyne, trans. *The Poetic Edda*. New York: Oxford University Press, 1996.

Simek, Rudolf, and Angela Hall, trans. *Norse Mythology: A Guide to the Gods, Heroes, Rituals, and Beliefs*. Rochester, NY: Boydell and Brewer, 2000.

Snorri Sturluson and Anthony Faulkes, trans. *Edda*. New York: Oxford University Press, 1991.

SEE ALSO: Aesir; Odin; Scandinavia; Titans; Ymir.

BLOOD

In all cultures around the world, blood has figured prominently in myth because of the connection between blood and life. Early civilizations may have had an understanding and awareness of blood different from the modern view. However, they recognized that too much blood loss leads to death and that blood is somehow connected to human fertility through menstruation.

Myths often use metaphors to explain underlying truths about life and the universe. For instance, myths can represent ideas of fertility and creation through the fluids that create or sustain life, such as blood. In many creation myths where the world is made by a male deity, for example, life is created by male blood falling on the earth, his blood impregnating the earth as semen impregnates a woman. In Egyptian mythology the gods Sia and Hu were created by drops of blood falling on the earth from Re's penis. The Greek Titans were likewise formed when Cronus castrated his father, Uranus, the sky god, causing his blood to fall on Gaia, the earth goddess. Also, in some Greek myths Aphrodite was created when Uranus's blood fell into the sea.

Blood and human creation myths

Divine blood also figured prominently in many human creation stories. According to the Yanomami of South America, humans arose when the moon's blood spilled onto the earth. The Koran teaches that humans were created from a blood clot inserted into clay. Similarly, the myths of Papua New Guinea, Japan, Mesopotamia, Mexico, and many other ancient civilizations explain the creation of humans as coming from a special clay produced by mixing dirt with divine blood.

Another potent quality of human blood was expressed by the ancient Scandinavians; that is, blood as divine inspiration for poetry. In the myth of Kvasir, one of the Vanir gods, two dwarves, Fjalar and Gjalar, murdered the god and mixed his blood with honey, allowing it to

Left: The two male figures in this fifth-century-BCE Greek ceramic bowl are preparing a boar for ritual sacrifice.

The Blood of the Greek Gods

In Greek mythology, a divine blood called ichor flowed through the veins and arteries of the Olympian gods. Ichor oozed from the deities' wounds in the same way that blood flows from mortals' cuts, but the loss of ichor did not kill a deity.

During the Trojan War Aphrodite experienced the loss of ichor when she was wounded by the mortal warrior Diomedes. In a battle that took place in the early years of the Trojan War, Prince Paris was wounded by Menelaus, king of Sparta and Helen's husband. Just at the point when Menelaus was about to kill Paris, Aphrodite, who loved the Trojan prince, encircled Paris in a heavy mist and began carrying him back to Helen's bedchamber. While the goddess was escaping through the ensuing battle, Diomedes, who was fighting furiously, slashed Aphrodite, spilling her ichor. During the same battle Aphrodite's lover, Ares, god of war, also lost ichor when he was wounded by a Greek warrior's spear.

Ichor was lost with more deadly consequences during the voyage of Jason and the Argonauts. When the adventurers attempted to approach the island of Crete, the giant bronze warrior Talos, who was guarding the island, hurled large boulders at the *Argo*, forcing back the ship. Ichor flowed through Talos's veins, which gave him strength and life. Only the sorceress Medea, who was in love with Jason and sailing with him aboard the *Argo*, knew how to stop Talos. She snuck to shore, cast a sleeping spell on the giant, and removed a nail at the giant's heel that plugged his veins. All his ichor oozed away and, not being a deity, the lifeless bronze giant fell into the sea. The story of Talos may symbolize the 1600 BCE volcanic eruption of Thera, which destroyed much of Crete.

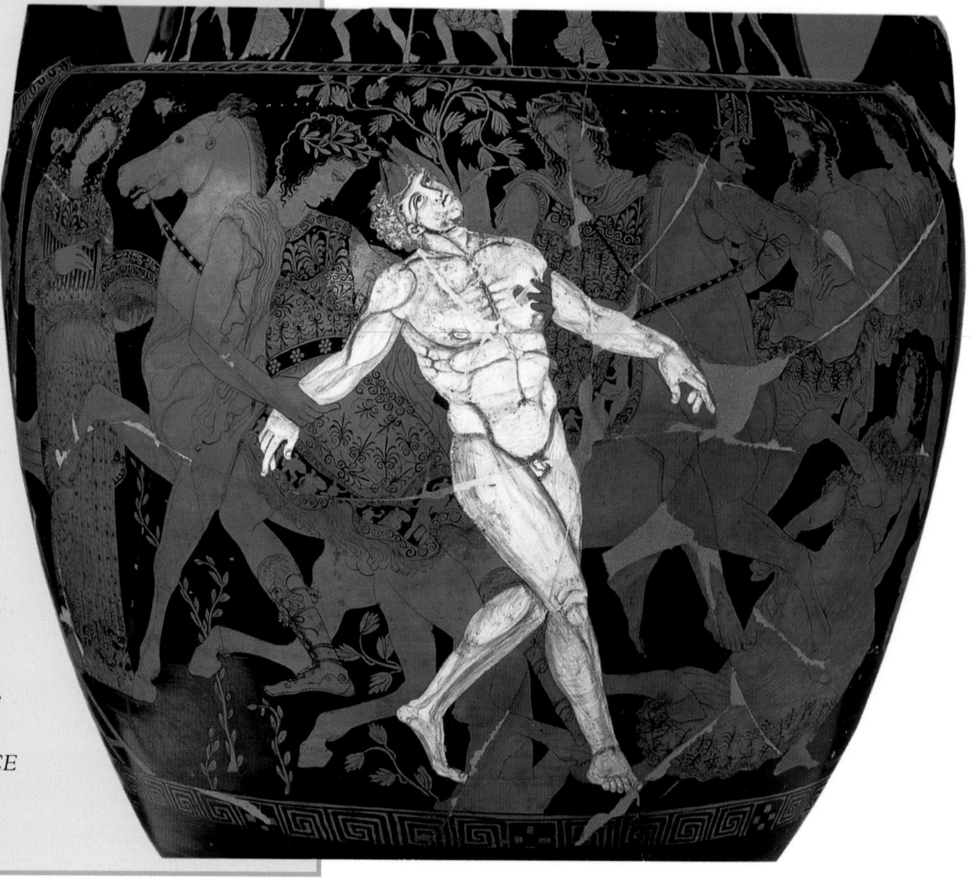

***Right:** The death of the bronze giant Talos is depicted in this fifth- or fourth-century-BCE pottery painting. Talos is the collapsing central white figure.*

ferment. This mixture became known as the "mead of poetry," a sip of which turned a person into an inspired poet. The connection between poetry and blood is also present in Irish folk belief, in which women dabbed the blood of the deceased on their lips to inspire the *keen,* an improvised lament for the dead.

Sacred practices and beliefs

In many cultures powerful substances are usually subject to taboos that govern how they are handled. Human blood is seen as being simultaneously pure and impure, sacred and profane, fertilizing and polluting. In some ancient civilizations certain priests or shamans were required to perform blood sacrifices, while in other cultures they were forbidden from ever touching or coming in contact with blood. Even today some religions continue a special treatment, or observation, of blood. The process of making meat kosher in Jewish law, for example, requires completely draining the blood from the slaughtered animal under the supervision and blessing of a rabbi. Hindu Brahmins, on the other hand, must never see blood at all.

There is also a widespread belief that land upon which human blood has fallen, especially the blood of a murder victim or menstrual blood, will be barren forever.

Above: A Roman carving of the god Mithras slaying a bull. This piece was found in London during an excavation in the late 19th century.

It was also believed that the wounds of a murder victim would begin to bleed afresh whenever the person's murderer was near. This belief is still held in many parts of the world today.

The Taurobolium

During the late Roman Empire, the West Asian deities Cybele and Mithras, who had been assimilated into the Roman pantheon, were very popular among the military and their families. Cybele was the Phrygian mother and fertility goddess. Male worshipers of Cybele castrated themselves, offering to the goddess both their semen and their blood. They also practiced self-flagellation, again offering their blood to the goddess. Female worshipers of Cybele practiced a ritual called the Taurobolium. In the Taurobolium, a bull was sacrificed by its throat being slit over a grate. The worshiper stood in a pit below the grate so that the bull's blood showered over her, drenching the worshiper and, it was believed, washing away all sins and personal impurities. Mithras was originally an Indo-Iranian god of regeneration and immortality who was widely worshiped in secret ceremonies by Roman soldiers. These soldiers adopted the Taurobolium as an important ritual in the worship of Mithras.

Human sacrifice

According to most mythologies from around the world, deities created life, and since blood is essential to life, the worship of gods often entailed offering blood to the creator deities as a way of thanking them for life. In some cultures the deities also relied on human blood for nourishment. In many ancient belief systems blood—animal or human—was the currency between humans and gods. Deities in some ancient civilizations enjoyed drinking blood. However, usually only blood freely given was acceptable as a sacrifice. In Greek sacrifices, for instance, grain was placed on the altar and the animal led to it. When the animal ate the grain, it was taken to mean that the animal acquiesced to its sacrifice.

Because of the physical dependence of life on blood, human blood was often conceived by ancient cultures as containing the soul or spirit of the person. When in Greek mythology Odysseus wished to consult the spirits of Hades, he had to sacrifice an animal and allow the spirits to drink its blood. Blood in this Greek example gave the bodiless spirits enough connection to the mortal, fleshy world to be able to produce voice and speech. In many places around the world, sacrifices to dead ancestors are still performed in such a way as to allow the blood to flow onto or into the grave in the belief that the blood will provide nourishment for the dead soul.

The Aztecs' gifts to the gods

In some cultures human sacrifice was reserved as a heavenly offering of last resort; in others, it was an ongoing ritual necessary to keep the gods satisfied and willing to bless the living. The best-known practitioners of human sacrifice were the Aztecs. Historians believe that at the time of first contact with Europeans in the early 16th century, the Aztecs were sacrificing thousands of people annually to their gods. Prisoners of war and hostages from vassal states were the preferred victims. They were brought to the tops of the pyramids, where their hearts were cut out and offered to the gods.

The Aztecs believed that the *tonalli* (animating spirit) was located in the blood, and that the blood concentrated in the heart when a person was in a state of terror. So the

Vampires

In the modern Western world the most widely known folkloric creature connected to blood is the vampire. Although the vampire has been present in the folklore of southeastern Europe for centuries, the creature gained widespread fame with the publication in 1897 of *Dracula*, a novel by the Anglo-Irish author Bram Stoker. This fame has been sustained by the appearance of the vampire in many films. According to legend, Stoker's book, and Hollywood, the vampire sucks the blood of the living, preferably of humans. By imbibing the blood and the life of others, the vampire becomes immortal, perishing only by having a stake thrust through its heart, by decapitation, or by having sunlight shone on it. In some versions of the legend, human vampires—known as "the undead"—are able to change into bats and fly. Vampires are also reputed to have no reflection, to abhor garlic, and to shrink from the sight of any Christian symbols, particularly crucifixes. To avoid the sun, they sleep by day in coffins.

Count Dracula is commonly but erroneously identified with Vlad Tepes (Vlad the Impaler), the 15th-century Romanian nationalist hero who fought the invading Turkish forces. He earned his byname by impaling his enemies on stakes while they were still alive. Vlad's castle at Bran in the Transylvanian Alps is now a popular tourist attraction for Westerners who have been captivated by the vampire legend.

Below: This still is from the 1931 Hollywood film Dracula, *in which Bela Lugosi, pictured here, stars as the vampire.*

Above: This illustration from a 16th-century Aztec codex shows a priest drawing blood from himself as part of a sacred offering to the gods.

heart of a terrified victim contained the most spirit and was the most valuable offering a god could be given. The Aztecs saw human sacrifice as an honor, and the victims of certain ceremonies were considered semidivine.

According to the writings of Julius Caesar (100–44 BCE), when the Romans conquered the Celtic realms of Gaul and Britain, they outlawed the druidic order, the priestly caste of the Celts, on the grounds that they practiced human sacrifice. The druids, according to Caesar, read omens in the way that the blood flowed from a sacrificial victim, seeing in it signs of the gods' will or the course of future events. For a while the druids tried to circumvent the ban by stabbing a victim but not killing him. This act provided the blood for the gods and the medium for reading the gods' intentions but was presented as a sacrifice of the blood rather than the human. Like the Aztecs, the druids supposedly preferred to sacrifice prisoners of war, people who were human but who did not share the same blood as the sacrificers.

Aboriginal blood-drinking ritual

For centuries in Australia the young men of Aboriginal groups drank human blood as a rite of passage from boyhood to adulthood. In the 19th century, when British missionaries were attempting to convert the Aborigines, many became interested in the Christian communion, particularly the drinking communion wine as a symbol of Christ's blood. The Aborigines saw this as an act very similar to their own ancient blood-drinking ritual.

In the Aboriginal blood-drinking ritual, the boy who was undergoing the ceremony was brought into a circle of male members of his group or clan and placed on the ground with his head on his father's thighs. The boy's father would cover the boy's eyes tightly. It was believed that if the boy witnessed any part of the ritual, both of the boy's parents would die. A wooden cup or bowl was given to the boy's uncle, who pierced his own arm and let the blood drip into the bowl. When finished, he would pass the bowl to the next man, who would repeat the action, and so on, until all the men had contributed blood to the bowl. The boy then had to drink all the blood in the bowl while the boy's father held the boy's throat to keep him from vomiting. It was believed that if the boy rejected any of the blood, then his parents, sisters, and brothers would all die. Sometimes the ritual continued for a whole month, during which the boy was allowed nothing to eat or drink except blood.

According to historians, earlier versions of the Aboriginal ritual were performed in which an older male member of the group was murdered. It was from him alone that the initiation blood was taken. Parts of the old man's corpse were also cut up and eaten. This was a symbolic reenactment of the eating of the primal father, another link with the Christian communion.

LESLIE ELLEN JONES

Bibliography

Clauss, Manfred, and Richard Gordon, trans. *The Roman Cult of Mithras: The God and His Mysteries*. New York: Routledge, 2001.

Davies, Nigel. *Human Sacrifice in History and Today*. New York: Morrow, 1981.

Ferguson, Diana. *Tales of the Plumed Serpent: Aztec, Inca and Mayan Myths*. New York: Sterling, 2000.

Green, Miranda. *Dying for the Gods: Human Sacrifice in Iron Age and Roman Europe*. London: Tempus Publishing, 2002.

Summer, Montague. *The Vampire in Lore and Legend*. New York: Dover Publications, 2001.

SEE ALSO: Aphrodite; Ares; Australia; Aztecs; Creation Myths; Crete; Cronus; Diomedes; Druids; Medea; Paris; Priests and Priestesses; Rites of Passage; Sacrifice; Uranus.

BOOK OF THE DEAD

Books of the dead are collections of magical spells that ancient Egyptians believed would enable them to reach a pleasant part of the next world after they died and to help them in the afterlife. The physical form of these writings varied—sometimes they were in a book placed in or near the coffin, sometimes they were inscriptions on the wall of the tomb. The most famous book of the dead was originally entitled The Book of Going Forth by Day. Several copies of this work have been preserved intact.

The Book of Going Forth by Day is the best-known book of the dead, but it is just one of many guides to the afterlife that were written in ancient Egypt. Others include The Book of What Is in the Underworld, The Book of Gates, The Book of Breathing, The Book of Caverns, The Spell of Twelve Gates, and The Book of the Earth.

Books of the dead were mainly either written on papyrus scrolls or inscribed on the walls of tombs. They were included in the burial arrangements of many wealthy Egyptians, including pharaohs, from about 1600 BCE. They were positioned close to the body, where the deceased would have the information close at hand, or at least be able to read it from where he or she lay. The spells they contained were intended to help the dead person accompany the sun god, Re, on his journey through the Duat, or underworld, to the afterlife.

Below: *The sun sets behind the pyramids of Giza. The daily journey of the sun played a central role in the religion of ancient Egypt.*

Above: *The interiors of many Egyptian tombs were decorated with paintings, magical spells, and other inscriptions to help the deceased on the journey to the afterlife. This tomb, at Saqqara, Egypt, was built between 2475 and 2467 BCE.*

The journey of the sun god

From the earliest times, ancient Egyptians believed that the sun god not only crossed the sky during the day, but also continued his journey during the hours of the night, traveling through a series of caverns or chambers beneath the earth. The disappearance of the sun below the horizon and the hours of darkness that followed were seen as a time when the sun might have died—no one could be sure of its fate until the next day's dawning.

The underworld was thought to be full of terror and danger, so the reappearance of the sun from its darkness was by no means a foregone conclusion. Therefore, dawn represented the victory of light and life over the forces of night, and it marked the rebirth of the sun god.

This continuing cycle was not only essential for the existence of life, but also offered a model in which death might not be the end for human beings. The many funerary texts of ancient Egypt all used the sun's daily journey as a metaphor for the religious belief that the death of the body—its passing into darkness—was not the end of existence, but would lead to a rebirth.

At the time when Egyptians were first building their pyramids, during a period known as the Old Kingdom (2575–2130 BCE), it was believed that only the king could accompany the sun god on his nightly travels. A collection of hymns and spells describing the journey was written in the covered roadways that led from the pyramids to the temples, and in a few of the underground chambers of the pyramids themselves. These are known as the Pyramid Texts; the oldest of them were written in about 2350 BCE.

The Pyramid Texts inspired many subsequent collections of spells, which were written on the insides of the square wooden coffins in which rich Egyptians were buried. These writings, called the Coffin Texts, first appeared in the ancient Egyptian Middle Kingdom around 1900 BCE. Like the Pyramid Texts, the Coffin Texts referred to the sun's journey through the sky; they also contained astronomical calculations and magical spells.

Unlike the Pyramid Texts, however, Coffin Texts were not just the exclusive privilege of semidivine kings, but were available to ordinary people—or at least to those who had the money to pay for the coffins, primarily officials and their subordinates. The coffins in which they were entombed became increasingly elaborate—they were shaped roughly like the wrapped mummies they contained and were decorated with spells, magical symbols, and pictures of the gods connected with the afterlife. These adornments were most commonly on the inside of the coffin but sometimes appeared on the outside, too.

By 1500 BCE, when the New Kingdom of ancient Egypt was beginning, the collected spells and hymns of the funerary ritual were increasingly written on papyrus rather than on wood. In addition to the writing, the books came to contain illustrations showing scenes of the underworld, magical symbols, or depictions of the dead person standing before Osiris, the god of the dead. Parts of these New Kingdom books of the afterlife also appeared on the walls of royal tombs or even inside the sarcophagi of kings and queens. Some tombs contained both papyrus rolls with spells and different versions of the texts on the walls, on coffins, and on other burial items. The papyrus might contain the most complete copy of an afterlife guidebook, while the tomb walls and coffins would be decorated with a selections of spells.

The Book of Going Forth by Day

Today the best known collection of spells is the Book of Going Forth by Day. Its various chapters concentrate on different ways of helping the deceased on their journey into the hereafter. Chapter 30, for example, contains a spell designed to prevent the dead person's heart from confessing before Osiris, and thus dooming his or her

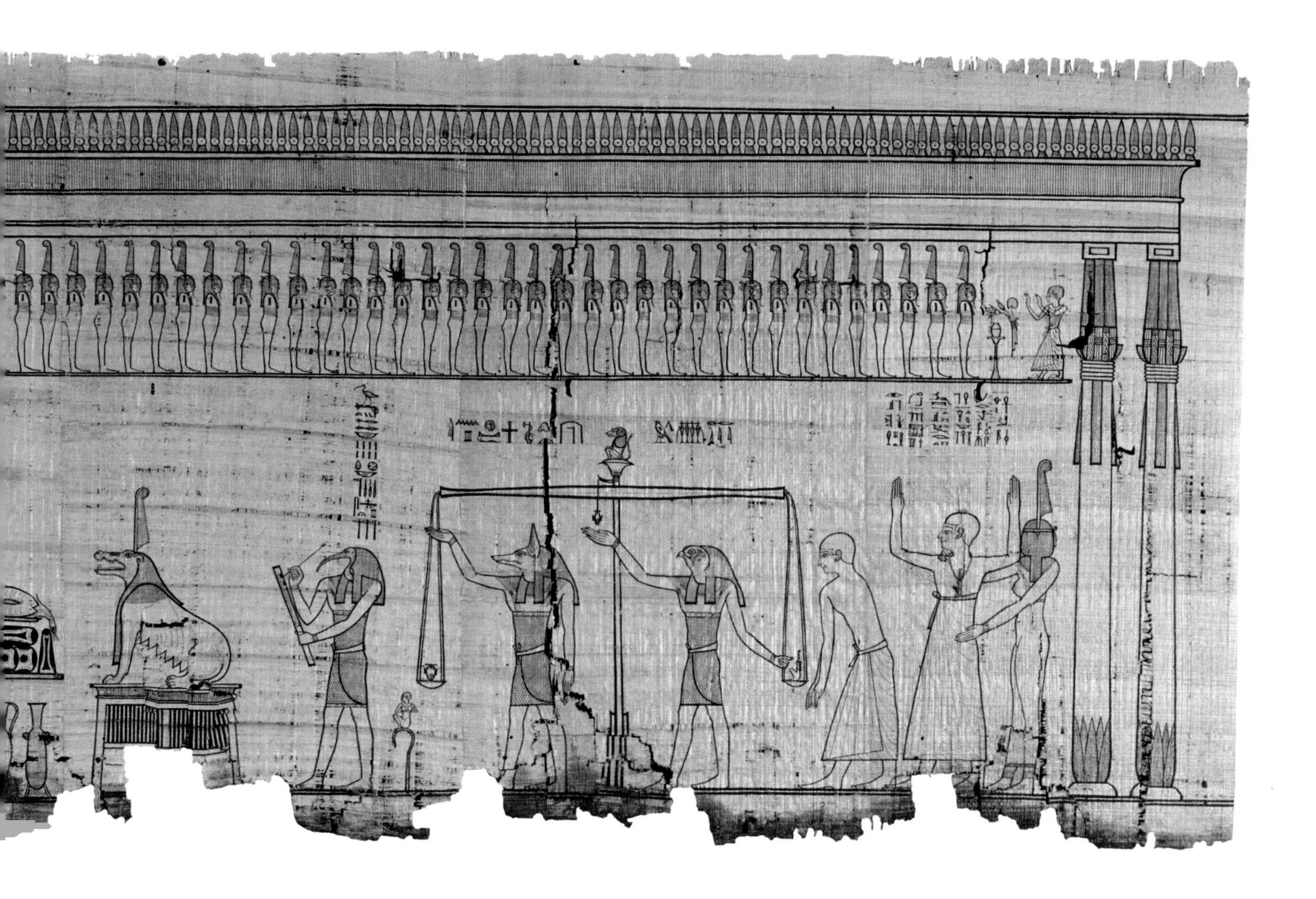

Above: This illustration from a book of the dead of the 14th century BCE shows the heart of a dead person being weighed in the afterlife.

soul to extinction. This spell was often written on amulets shaped like winged scarab beetles and placed over the heart of the mummy. The acts that could condemn the soul were listed in section 125 of the Book of Going Forth by Day, sometimes known alternatively as The Negative Confession. These crimes included killing, stealing, lying, and cheating. However, other, less serious misdeeds were also mentioned as possibly leading to damnation. These included bullying people, being bad-tempered, gossiping, or even talking too much. In the presence of Osiris, it was important neither to admit too much nor to give the god reason to doubt that you were telling the truth. Therefore the texts often outlined an appropriate set of formal responses that would allay suspicion.

While most of the Pyramid Texts and the Coffin Texts were similar in content, few versions were exactly identical. There were two reasons for this. One was that each book was transcribed by hand—there was no printing or other form of mass reproduction, so inconsistencies were bound to appear through scribal errors. The other reason was that, when rich people died, they might have one of several collections of spells drawn up, personalized with their name and even their portrait.

Hieratic Writing

Pyramid Texts and Coffin Texts were written in hieroglyphs (writing that uses pictures or symbols to represent ideas, rather than sounds). So, too, were the later guides to the afterlife on tomb walls. However, the papyrus copies of these books were often written partly in formal hieroglyphs and partly in hieratic writing.

Hieratic writing is a form of hieroglyphs in which the hieroglyphic signs are simplified for easy writing, much as modern cursive changes the shapes of letters of the alphabet so that they are quicker to write. While hieroglyphs are easily identified as pictures of animals, people, gods, or other objects, hieratic writing is more abstract. It may have been developed so that scribes could make copies of the books more quickly for their customers. Some of the books might also have been prepared by two or more people: one to write out the long text, and the other to draw the elaborate illustrations. The word *hieratic* means "relating to priests," and it was these holy men—the only literate people in society—who made the transcriptions.

Although most of the writing on papyrus was done in plain black ink, the first line of each spell or group of spells might be done in red. The accompanying illustrations were often beautifully drawn and colored. Some even had pieces of gold leaf on crowns or jewelry worn by the figures of gods and humans.

These collections of spells became very popular, and in response to the great demand, scribes even started to turn out premade copies with blank spaces for the individual customer's name to be inscribed. We know about this practice because the scribes were occasionally in such a hurry that they forgot to fill in the blanks, a serious mistake that could have invalidated some of the spells.

The Book of What Is in the Underworld was first inscribed on the walls of a king's tomb about 1550 BCE, but it was probably composed some time before that. It promised to impart the knowledge of the underworld, and described the journey of the sun god through the twelve hours of the night, complete with his speeches, actions, and interactions with other beings of the underworld. Since the sun god would "die" at sunset, it was his soul *(Ba)* that would make the journey. It would later be reunited with his body so that he could be reborn at first light on the following morning.

Before all this could happen, however, the soul of the sun god would have to overcome a dangerous enemy. This enemy, called Apophis (or Apop), took the form of a giant snake, which tried to stop the sun from completing the journey. Many gods and goddesses were summoned to help neutralize this danger and to aid in the revival of the sun god. The underworld also contained many other marvels and dangers, including a lake of fire. Human beings whose souls made the journey with the sun could hope to be reborn into a perfect existence.

As well as the Book of Going Forth by Day and the Book of What Is in the Underworld, several other books of this type were equally popular in ancient Egypt. The oldest surviving copies of The Spell of the Twelve Gates date from the reign of Amenhotep II (1450–1425 BCE), and the text continued to be copied for more than a thousand years. Like the Book of What Is in the Underworld, the Spell of the Twelve Gates contains

Ushabtis and Shawabtis

The magic spells from the Book of Going Forth by Day were not only written on papyrus scrolls. Important spells were also found on amulets and items of funerary furniture. Other spells were written on little servant figures called ushabtis before the 21st dynasty, which ended in 945 BCE, and after that on shawabtis or shabtis. In ancient Egypt pharaohs were often buried with the bodies of their servants, who were expected to perform tasks for their masters in the afterlife. Ordinary Egyptians did not have this luxury. Instead they were buried with carved figurines inscribed with Chapter 6 of the Book of Going Forth by Day. This spell was intended to make them come alive and work in place of the dead person in the afterlife. Hundreds of ushabtis could be buried in a single tomb. They were first buried with the dead during the Middle Kingdom and continued to be popular until after the conquest of Egypt by Macedonia in 332 BCE.

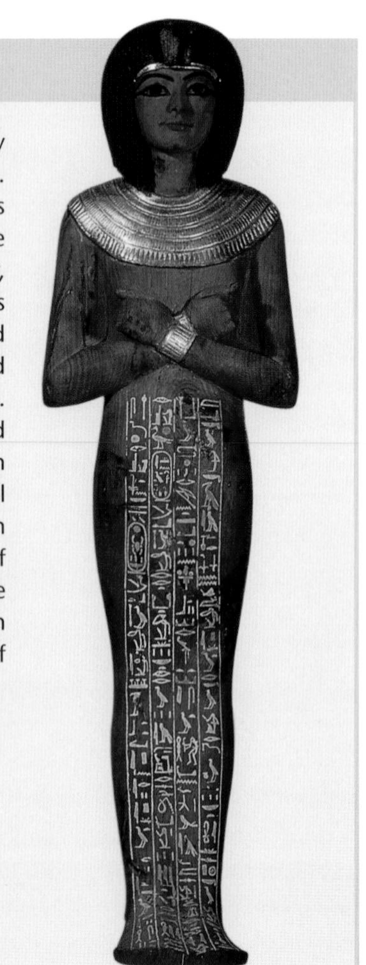

Left and right: *Treasures from the tomb of Tutankhamen. These two statuettes, made in about 1340 BCE and buried with the body of the ancient Egyptian boy king, are some of the latest surviving examples of ushabtis. They were intended to do agricultural work for the monarch in the afterlife.*

Above: The interior of this ancient Egyptian sarcophagus (ornamental tomb) was richly decorated.

descriptions of the caves of the underworld. Each cave corresponded to a different hour of the night during which different groups of gods and goddesses appeared.

The earliest complete copy of The Book of Gates comes from about 1300 BCE, just after the reign of King Tutankhamen (1361–1352 BCE). It became one of the most popular guidebooks to the afterlife in royal tombs, but no two copies are exactly the same. From its title, the Book of Gates sounds as if it would be very similar to the collections of spells just mentioned, but its contents are in fact more like the chapters of the Book of What Is in the Underworld. In the Book of Gates, the twelve hours of the night are set out very systematically. More than a thousand gods and deceased persons are mentioned in the various surviving versions of the text.

The Book of Caverns had a number of original sections that dealt with the punishments that would be meted out in the afterlife to enemies of the sun god and of the dead king. These unfortunates were condemned to the Place of Annihilation, from which there was no escape. There they were immersed in heated cauldrons or tortured. According to the text, evildoers were held upside down, suspended forever in primeval darkness, so that they could neither see nor hear the sun god. They were also robbed of their *Ba* (souls). Many aspects of these punishment scenes are similar to depictions of Hell in other religions.

Several different versions of the afterlife guides continued to be copied even after the Roman conquest of Egypt in 30 BCE. By then funerary texts had a long history, and the tradition was firmly established. They continued to gain adherents because they served important purposes. They gave people some idea of what they might encounter in the afterlife, both good and bad; they offered ways of ensuring that the good came to pass and the bad could be overcome; and they promised a means by which human beings could live eternally.

LYN GREEN

Bibliography

Faulkner, Raymond, trans. *The Egyptian Book of the Dead: The Book of Going Forth by Day.* San Francisco, CA: Chronicle Books, 2000.

Hobson, Christine. *The World of the Pharaohs.* New York: Thames and Hudson, 1990.

SEE ALSO: Atum; Death and the Afterlife; Egypt; Osiris; Re.

BOR

In Norse mythology Bor was the son of Búri, the first god, and an important figure in the Norse creation story. He was also the father of Odin, the powerful patriarch of the gods. Beyond that, however, few references to or myths about Bor exist.

Above: Bor's most important role in Norse mythology was as the father of Odin, chief of the gods, illustrated here sitting on his throne in Asgard.

One of the most ancient Norse gods, Bor was wrapped in snow, mist, and mystery. Almost nothing is known about him except that he was part of the Norse creation story. In the poem *Völuspá* ("The Seeress's Prophecy"), written around 1000 CE, Odin called up a seeress from Niflheim, the underworld, to tell the gods stories of how the world was made and how it would be destroyed. In these stories Odin's father, Bor, played a small but crucial part.

In the beginning there was a great void called Ginnungagap, which lay at the center of what would become heaven and earth. To the south was a fiery region and to the north was a desolate land of ice. In the middle of Ginnungagap, where fire and ice met, a gigantic being rose in a rush of steam. Ymir was his name, and he drank the milk of a cow named Audhumla. While Ymir suckled Audhumla's udder, the cow licked a block of ice. Out of the ice emerged Búri, who became the ancestor of all the gods. Soon after, from one of Ymir's legs emerged Thrúdgelmir, an ugly six-headed frost giant who would later become the father of Bergelmir, who in turn would become father of the giants.

Scholars believe that Audhumla originally represented the importance of cattle to the early Germanic-speaking peoples who probably originated in the Trans-Volga region around 4000 BCE and then migrated across Eastern Europe to Scandinavia, England, and eventually as far as Iceland. Cattle were the source of wealth for these nomadic people, and many fabled battles were fought among the Norse, Celts, and other Germanic tribes over cattle stealing. Because she brought Búri into existence, Audhumla was the mother of gods and men.

Búri had a son named Bor, who grew up to marry Bestla, the daughter of a frost giant—an ironic connection since Bor's sons grew up to kill many of their mother's relatives. Bor and Bestla had three sons, Odin, Vili, and Vé. Odin, Bor's eldest son, became king of the gods and ruler of Asgard, home of the gods. The younger two were less well known. All three attacked the frost giant Ymir and hacked him to pieces, drowning the world in his blood.

Frigga betrays Odin

In another myth Frigga, Odin's wife, took Vili and Vé as lovers during Odin's absence, an act that caused tension among the three brothers. Odin had trusted Vili and Vé to rule in his place while he traveled, but they took both his wife and his kingdom. It is not stated what Odin did to his brothers when he came back from his journeys, but it is implied that he dealt with the usurpers harshly.

BARBARA GARDNER

Bibliography

Larrington, Carolyne, trans. *The Poetic Edda.* New York: Oxford University Press, 1996.

Lindow, John. *Norse Mythology: A Guide to the Gods, Heroes, Rituals, and Beliefs.* New York: Oxford University Press, 2002.

SEE ALSO: Animals; Bergelmir; Búri; Frigga; Odin; Scandinavia; Ymir.

BRITOMARTIS

According to Greek mythology, Britomartis was born half mortal and half divine and was transformed into a goddess of nature and the sea. Mainly associated with the island of Crete, Britomartis became integrated into the family of Olympian gods, who were worshiped across ancient Greece. She was also a member of Artemis's band of huntresses. Britomartis's name means "sweet maiden," and she was depicted in art and literature as a young woman.

According to most Greek mythological sources, Britomartis was the daughter of Carme (also spelled Karme), a mortal woman, and Zeus, king of the gods. One source has Carme as the daughter of Euboulos, who may have been an agricultural deity. Like many half-divine figures, such as Heracles, Britomartis began life as a mortal and then became a god. As a young woman, she joined the band of virgin huntresses who gathered in the wilderness around Artemis, goddess of the hunt. Britomartis swore an oath to Artemis that she would remain a virgin and live forever in the woods, remaining loyal to the goddess.

One day Minos, king of Crete, Britomartis's birthplace, saw Britomartis and fell deeply in love with her. He chased the young woman through the wilderness until he cornered her on the seashore. Trapped, Britomartis jumped into a fisherman's net that was being lowered into the sea. According to one version of the story, Artemis then saved Britomartis from drowning by transforming her into a goddess. In another version Britomartis hid in the net and sailed with the fisherman to Aegina, an island near Athens. When she saw that Minos had sailed after her, Britomartis fled to a grove that was sacred to Artemis. Artemis then took Britomartis away and made her a goddess.

Interpretations of the myth

A number of Greek myths tell of a young woman who was pursued by either a king, hero, or god and lost her human form while trying to escape. Daphne, for example, was changed into a tree in order to protect her from the attentions of Apollo. This pattern can be explained in terms of the transformation of girls into women. In many cultures young people go into the wilderness for initiation into adulthood. In ancient Greece the initiation of girls often took place outside the community during religious rites devoted to Artemis, who was known as the virgin goddess of wild places.

From the perspective of acknowledging the rite of passage from childhood to adulthood, Britomartis's story can be interpreted as a failed initiation, since she refused to leave the wilderness to become a wife and mother, as was expected of women. It may also be significant that, in one account, Minos pursued her for nine months—the human gestation period. Some scholars even interpret the myth of Britomartis as a young woman's reluctance to undergo marriage and childbirth.

Britomartis's story is also instructive about the fusion and differences of religious beliefs throughout the many city-states and island cultures of Greece. Britomartis's myth may have expanded over time to include aspects of similar goddesses in later cultures, or her story may have taken on local attributes as her myth and her worship spread throughout the region. The people of Aegina, for example, worshiped the goddess Aphaea (or Aphaia), whose name means "taken away," as in Britomartis's disappearance from Artemis's grove. Similarly, Cretans worshiped the goddess Dictynna, whose name, in reference to one version of Britomartis's myth, means "net." Some scholars believe that Aphaea and Dictynna were not separate goddesses but are actually different names for Britomartis or, at the very least, different aspects of the same goddess.

Minoan roots

As far back as the Middle Bronze Age (roughly 2000–1500 BCE), Aegina shared cultural ties with the Minoans, a pre-Greek civilization centered on Crete and named for the mythical king Minos who pursued Britomartis. Since the Greeks absorbed and were much influenced by Minoan

Above: This temple to Britomartis still stands on the Greek island of Aegina, where the goddess was known as Aphaea.

culture during the Late Bronze Age (roughly 1500–1100 BCE), Britomartis, Dictynna, and Aphaea may be related to a goddess of the wilderness who featured prominently in Minoan mythology. Later Greeks seem to have associated all three goddesses with the Olympian family through the figure of Artemis, who was not herself worshiped in the Bronze Age but was sometimes called Dictynna.

Historical references

In addition to adopting Minoan deities, the Greeks also inherited some ancient Minoan rituals, such as making offerings and praying at shrines that were dedicated to Britomartis. The remains of one of Britomartis's shrines can still be seen on Aegina. At least some of these shrines featured wooden statues of the goddess. The image on display at Olous on Crete, for example, was said to have been carved by the legendary master craftsman Daedalus. Britomartis's name also appears in Cretan documents of the seventh century BCE and later inscribed in stone, which suggests that she was sometimes connected with the official Greek religion.

Worship of Britomartis does not seem to have spread much beyond Crete and Aegina, nor is she well represented in ancient Greek art and literature. Nevertheless, her story continued to inspire poets, such as Alexandrine Callimachus, a Greek writer of the third century BCE, and Ciris, a Roman writer of the first century BCE. Other sources include the eighth-century-BCE Greek poet Hesiod and, during Roman times, the Greek historians Strabo (c. 64 BCE–23 CE) and Pausanias (fl. 143–176 CE), both of whom explored the geography and history of ancient Greece. References to Britomartis were also made by the Roman poet Virgil (70–19 BCE), and archaeologists have discovered ancient coins with images of the goddess.

JIM MARKS

Bibliography

Edwards, Ruth B. *Kadmos the Phoenician: A Study in Greek Legends and the Mycenean Age*. Amsterdam: Hakkert, 1979.

Farnaux, Alexandre, and David J. Baker, trans. *Knossos: Searching for the Legendary Palace of King Minos*. New York: Harry N. Abrams, 1996.

Graves, Robert. *The Greek Myths*. New York: Penguin USA, 1993.

SEE ALSO: Apollo; Artemis; Callisto; Crete; Daedalus; Daphne; Minos; Virginity; Zeus.

BÚRI

In Old Norse mythology Búri was the first god and grandfather of Odin, head of the gods. Even though this was an important mythological role, little is known about Búri because he appeared so rarely in myths. There are even some scholars who argue that Búri was not a god but a giant.

Búri (or Buri) was the ancestor of the gods in Norse mythology. What little information scholars have found about him comes from the Norse creation myth. He was the father of Bor and the grandfather of Odin, chief of the gods, and Odin's brothers, Vili and Vé. The primary source for Búri is the *Prose Edda*, a mythological guidebook written in about 1220 by the Icelandic scholar and historian Snorri Sturluson (1179–1241) and intended for skalds (court poets).

Some scholars interpret Búri's name as meaning "progenitor" and relate it to Old Norse *bera*, "to bear" or "to carry," or alternatively, "to dwell" from the word *búa*. Another possible origin might be the north Norwegian word *bura*, which means "to bellow" or "to roar." This interpretation would mean that Búri was a giant rather than a god because roaring was directly associated with Old Norse giants, not gods. However, the text of the *Prose Edda* does not give any indication of whether Búri was actually believed to have been a giant or a god.

Mythic origin of Búri

According to the creation story, the universe first existed only as a great void, called Ginnungagap (meaning "vast magic space" or "void"), which lay between Niflheim, the cold regions of the north (also the underworld), and Muspel, the hot regions of the south. Where fire and ice met inside the gap, two primeval creatures came into being: the frost giant Ymir (also known as Aurgelmir) and the cow Audhumla (sometimes called Audumla or Audhumbla). The cow's name means "the hornless cow with lots of milk" and comes from the Old Norse words *audr* ("riches" or "wealth") and *humla* ("hornless").

Below: *The harsh yet majestic mountains in Galdhopiggen, Norway, served in part as inspiration for Búri and other Old Norse gods.*

Above: This painting by Danish artist N. A. Abildgaard (1743–1809) shows Audhumla licking Búri into existence and giving milk to Ymir.

The cow nursed Ymir with her milk while she licked the salty ice blocks for nourishment. After one day of licking she had freed Búri's hair from the ice, after the second day his head was visible, and after the third Búri was completely uncovered from the ice. (There is some ambiguity in the translation of the text as to whether the cow only licks away the ice or actually sculpts Búri from the ice.) The *Prose Edda* does not give a lot of information on Búri's physical appearance other than that he was beautiful, big, and powerful. Búri had a son called Bor, but nothing is said about Bor's mother. Bor himself had three sons, Odin, Vili ("the Will"), and Vé ("the Shrine" or "the Sacred One"), by the giantess Bestla, daughter of Bölthorn.

Searching for sources

The myth of Búri is seldom mentioned in any other Old Norse source and is not included at all in any of the poems contained in the *Poetic Edda* (also called *Elder Edda*), a collection of mythological and heroic stories found in a single manuscript, the Codex Regius, which dates from the 1270s and is now kept in Reykjavík, Iceland.

Also Búri and Bor, as ancestors of Odin, do not appear in Old English (Anglo-Saxon) royal genealogies, as do some of the other Old Norse gods. However, a 10th-century verse by the Norse court poet Egill Skallagrímsson provides evidence that the tradition of Bor as father of Odin goes back to an ancient tradition in Scandinavia. Even so, the verse does not mention Búri as the father of Bor.

Finally, although Búri was the ancestor of the gods, he does not seem to have been worshiped much, and historians have not identified any cults associated with him.

DONATA KICK

Bibliography

Lindow, John. *Norse Mythology: A Guide to the Gods, Heroes, Rituals, and Beliefs*. New York: Oxford University Press, 2002.

Snorri Sturluson, and Anthony Faulkes, trans. *Edda*. London: Everyman, 1995.

SEE ALSO: Bor; Odin; Scandinavia.

CADMUS

Cadmus was the legendary founder of Thebes and was credited with bringing the alphabet to ancient Greece. He also married Harmonia, the daughter of Ares and Aphrodite, and toward the end of their lives both were transformed into snakes.

According to legend, Cadmus (or Kadmos) was a Phoenician from the ancient city of Tyre, which still exists in modern Lebanon. The main source for the story of Cadmus is *The Library,* a collection of Greek myths attributed to Apollodorus, a writer who lived some time in the first two centuries CE. Cadmus was the grandson of Poseidon, god of the sea. His parents were Agenor, king of Phoenicia, and Telephassa, a Phoenician princess, and he had two brothers, Phoenix and Cilix, and a sister, Europa.

The search for Europa

The story of the founding of Thebes began when Zeus, ruler of the gods, disguised himself as a bull and abducted Europa. Agenor ordered his sons to search for her and not return until she was found. Each brother set off in a different direction. Phoenix looked throughout Phoenicia, Cilix went to Cilicia, and Thasus (Cilix's son who joined in the search) traveled to the island of Thasus. Eventually all gave up the search. Since each of them had failed to find Europa, they were forbidden to return home, and so they settled in the areas where they had been searching.

Cadmus had visited the islands of Rhodes, Samothrace, Thera, and Thrace before landing in Greece, where he continued to search for his sister. He arranged a meeting with the oracle at Delphi, who was supposedly able to see into the future and be all knowing, to ask where he could find Europa.

The oracle told him to abandon the search, since Zeus did not want her to be found. Instead the oracle told Cadmus to look for a cow and follow it until it lay down in weariness. On the spot where the cow lay he was to found and fortify a city. The Greek travel writer Pausanias, who lived in the second century CE, wrote that the oracle told Cadmus that the cow must have a moon-shaped mark

Right: *The colorful painting inside this Italian ornamental ceramic cup depicts the transformation of Cadmus and his wife, Harmonia, into snakes.*

Above: In this early-20th-century book illustration, the young Cadmus confronts a dragon before founding the city of Thebes. The illustration, by artist Virginia Frances Sterrett, is in a volume of mythological stories titled Tanglewood Tales.

Cadmus and the Greek Alphabet

Herodotus, a Greek historian who lived during the fifth century BCE, credited Cadmus with bringing the Phoenician alphabet to Greece. Although the alphabet that was used by the Greeks in Herodotus's time was indeed descended from the Phoenicians, the alphabet was not nearly as old as Thebes. Archaeologists believe that Thebes was occupied around 3000 BCE, in the Early Bronze Age. During the Late Bronze Age, around 1600 BCE, the Greeks had a writing system known as Linear B. It was adapted from the Minoan script, known as Linear A, used by the inhabitants of Crete. Linear A was actually not an alphabet but a syllabary: each symbol represented a combination of a consonant and a vowel, rather than a single sound. The system fell into disuse around 1100 BCE.

In the eighth century BCE the Greeks began to use the Phoenician alphabet (the one Cadmus is credited with introducing). In this writing system each symbol represented a single sound. The Greeks modified the Phoenician system, changing the shapes of some of the letters and adding vowels, since the original Phoenician alphabet represented only consonants. The Etruscans, who lived in Italy, borrowed the Greek alphabet and modified it again. The Romans, who conquered the Etruscans, adopted the Etruscan alphabet and made some slight variations. The Roman alphabet is used in most of the Western world today.

on each side of its body. When Cadmus left the oracle he saw just such a cow and followed it through the land of Phocis, near Delphi, and into Boeotia, in central Greece. Finally, the cow lay down to rest and Cadmus sacrificed it to Athena, goddess of war and wisdom. Centuries later Pausanias claimed to be able to identify the shrine to Athena said to have been built by Cadmus.

The rise of the *Spartoi*

After sacrificing the cow, Cadmus sent his men to a nearby spring to draw water. The guardian of the spring, a huge and ferocious serpent or dragon, killed most of Cadmus's men. The dragon was a servant of Ares, god of war. Cadmus, unaware of what had happened, went to the spring to look for his men. He found the bodies of his servants with the giant serpent looming over them. Cadmus slew the serpent. Afterward Athena told Cadmus to remove the beast's teeth and plant them in the ground (Jason did the same thing with the teeth of the dragon that guarded the Golden Fleece). From the buried teeth immediately grew fierce, fully armed warriors, who began fighting each other. When the fighting stopped, five of the warriors survived. The warriors—Echion, Udaeus, Chthonius, Hyperenor, and Pelorus—were known as the *Spartoi,* meaning the "sown men." With the help of the *Spartoi,* Cadmus built a mighty palace and laid the foundation for Thebes, which became one of the major city-states in ancient Greece and was the setting for the story of Oedipus. Some scholars have suggested that the myth of Cadmus's founding of Thebes represents the city's actual historical association with Phoenicia (see box).

Cadmus's marriage and transformation

Another tale in the life of Cadmus involved his marriage to the goddess Harmonia, daughter of Ares and Aphrodite. The Olympian gods attended the wedding feast, and the Muses, nine daughters of Zeus who were associated with the arts, sang for the guests. Hephaestus, god of fire and metalworking, gave the couple a necklace and a robe, and some sources say that the other gods gave gifts as well. Pausanias wrote that in his time (c. 160 CE) the Thebans could identify the ruins of Cadmus's palace, Harmonia's wedding chamber, and the spot where the Muses sang.

Cadmus and Harmonia had four daughters: Agave, Ino, Autonoe, and Semele. Some sources say that they had a son, Polydorus, although Euripides, a fifth-century-BCE Athenian playwright, wrote in his play the *Bacchants*—or *Bacchae*—that Cadmus had no sons. Cadmus's daughter Semele bore the god Dionysus to Zeus, but all his other grandchildren died in tragic circumstances before marriage.

According to Ovid, a Roman poet of the first century CE, Cadmus and Harmonia went to Illyria after the tragic death of their grandchildren, where they were turned into snakes. One version explains that the couple's transformation was in revenge for Cadmus's having killed the giant serpent at the spring. Pindar, a Theban poet of the fifth century BCE, wrote that Cadmus and Harmonia joined Peleus, Achilles, and other mortals in the Elysian Fields, where they lived forever. In the *Bacchae*, Euripides seems to combine several myths, saying that the couple left Thebes, became snakes, and were finally brought to the Elysian Fields.

LAUREL BOWMAN

Bibliography

Edwards, Ruth B. *Kadmos the Phoenician: A Study in Greek Legends and the Mycenean Age.* Amsterdam: Hakkert, 1979.

Euripides, and Paul Roche, trans. *10 Plays.* New York: Signet Classic, 1998.

SEE ALSO: Aphrodite; Ares; Athena; Dragons; Europa; Oedipus.

CALENDARS

For over 10,000 years humans have relied on calendars to predict seasonal changes. This was important because ancient civilizations needed to anticipate and keep track of when to plant and harvest crops. In many civilizations the calendar was also tied closely to the deities that they believed controlled the cycle of the seasons or the movement of the heavens. Rituals and ceremonies needed to take place on specific dates to honor certain gods. Because charting the changing of seasons was so vital to ancient civilizations, many cultures assigned deities to most or all units of the calendar, from days to decades.

Archaeologists have discovered systems of time recognition and dating from the earliest known period of writing. Over the centuries ancient civilizations developed calendars that suited their environment and were usually based on celestial observations. Most calendars are determined by the cycles of the moon (months), the revolutions of the earth around the sun (years), and in some cases the position of the stars.

Calendar of ancient Egypt

Over centuries the Egyptians developed three calendars that ran concurrently. The first was for agriculture, the second for administrative purposes, and the third for religious festivals.

Right: *The Chinese zodiac calendar, such as this one, which combines Buddhist symbols in the inner ring with zodiac signs in the outer ring, was invented many centuries ago. The ancient Chinese were highly accomplished astronomers and mathematicians and based their calendars on the movements of the stars. However, they also applied religious significance to their celestial observations, as indicated by the Buddhist symbols here.*

The first calendar was based on the cycles of the moon, giving 12 months in each year, and the annual appearance of Sirius at dusk. Sirius, also called the Dog Star, is the brightest star in the night sky and part of the constellation Canis Major. The appearance of Sirius was important to ancient Egyptians because it heralded the annual flooding of the Nile. Archaeologists have discovered evidence of this calendar dating to 4236 BCE.

The first calendar was flawed, however, because the 12 cycles of the moon did not match the actual annual sightings of Sirius. In an attempt to reconcile the discrepancy, a second, civil calendar was created. It was made up of 365 days for each year: 12 months of 30 days each, and an additional five days added at the end of the year. Because the second calendar was not anchored to any celestial event, it actually ended up being short by one full day every four years when compared to the solar year.

The change from the first to the second calendar is detailed in the following myth from ancient Egypt. Atum, the creator god, forbade Geb (father earth) and Nut (mother sky) from mating. They disregarded him and Nut became pregnant. Angry, Atum decreed that Nut would bear her offspring "in no month of the year." Nut, heavy with child and in distress, sought the help of Thoth, who engaged the Moon in a dice game for a prize of five additional days. Thoth won the game and gave the five extra days to Nut, who then bore her child within those days because they fell "in no month of the year."

Most Egyptians found the discrepancy between the two calendars confusing. To solve the problem, a third calendar was created, but this time not based on the appearance of Sirius. Although it was again based on the cycles of the moon, it inserted an extra month whenever the new year fell before the first day of the civil (second) calendar. This insertion of days or months to regularize a calendar over long periods of time is called intercalation. In our modern calendar, February 29, which occurs only in leap years, is an intercalation.

Babylonian dating system

Some centuries after the Egyptians, the Babylonians, a great civilization located in modern Iraq, observed a 12-month solar year that was divided into two seasons. Neighboring civilizations to the north, such as the Assyrians and the Anatolians, recognized three or four seasons, depending on their climate.

The Babylonian new year began with the harvest of barley, their primary crop, during which the king would offer fruits to the gods. As in early Egypt, there was a calendar for agriculture, a calendar for administration, and a calendar for religious and royal usage. However, the royal calendar was very haphazard. Because the months failed to

Below: These modern Egyptian fishermen, like their ancestors thousands of years ago, rely on the seasonal predictions offered by calendars to tell them when the Nile River will experience its high-water season, the optimum time of year for fishing.

match the seasons, the king would often decree a new month to be inserted into a particular year. This capricious system lasted until 300 BCE, when the Babylonians began using a 19-year cycle in which the solar year matched the two seasons and the calendar months started with each new moon. Aspects of Babylonian timekeeping were adopted by other cultures. For example, their day began at sunset, an observance still practiced by Jews, and their belief in the sacredness of the number seven, led to the seven-day week.

Above: Copied from a ceiling painting in the Temple of Hathor, built in Egypt in the fourth century BCE, the figures in this artwork represent the seasonal and daily divisions of an Egyptian calendar.

The Chinese calendar

Archaeologists have discovered evidence of a lunar-solar calendar in use in China as far back as the 14th century BCE. The ancient Chinese had a highly sophisticated calendar. It was based on careful astronomical observations and the plotting of both the sun and the moon, which greatly aided farmers and cultivation. They believed that a reliable, well-ordered calendar symbolized a good relationship between heaven and the imperial court. Over the centuries several methods of intercalation were used, including adding a month every 19 years.

The Chinese named each year for one of the 12 animals of the zodiac. These were the rat, ox, tiger, rabbit, dragon, snake, horse, sheep, monkey, rooster, dog, and pig (or boar).

This sequence was traditionally assigned according to the following myth. One day, the 12 animals fought over precedence in the cycle of years in the calendar. The Chinese gods held a contest to see which animal should be first. The animals lined up on a riverbank and were told to swim across the river. The first to arrive on the opposite bank would get the first year, and the order would continue sequentially. The 12 animals jumped in the river. The rat snuck up and climbed on the ox's back. Just as the ox came ashore, the rat jumped off and finished the race first. The lazy pig arrived last. So the rat got the first year named after him, the ox got the second year, and the pig ended up with the last year in the cycle. At the end of 12 years the naming sequence started again.

Calendar of India

Scholars believe that the ancient Hindu calendar, the primary calendar of India, started around 1000 BCE and was based on 12 lunar months plus an intercalation of an extra month every 30 months. In fact, the ancient Hindus used several calendars. Three of the most influential were the Vikram Samvat, the Yugabdha, and the Vedic. The

Below: *Dragon lanterns such as this feature in Chinese New Year celebrations around the world. The origins of the practice are said to lie in the myth of the emperor's servant girl, Yuan Xiao.*

The Lantern Festival

The Lantern Festival is the climax of Chinese New Year celebrations. The Lantern Festival reflects a myth from long ago. A girl named Yuan Xiao worked as a lowly servant in the Chang-an palace of Emperor Wu Di of the Han Dynasty. She was intelligent, full of kindness in her heart, and had many friends. She longed to visit her family, yet was not allowed to leave the palace grounds. A minister called Shuo Dong Fang befriended Yuan Xiao and thought up a plan to distract the emperor so that she could leave the palace secretly and visit her family. Shuo informed the emperor that the Supreme Deity of Heaven had ordered the God of Fire to burn the city of Chang-an to the ground on the 16th day of the lunar year. Shuo said that the way to avert this disaster was to set off firecrackers, flood the city streets with red lanterns, and require all palace maids to take lanterns and parade in the streets. Shuo recommended that Yuan Xiao present dumplings to the God of Fire; once he was satiated, the city would be spared. So it was that the emperor ordered the city of Chang-an to keep busy that entire night, setting off firecrackers and playing with lanterns. Yuan Xiao took advantage of the confusion to escape the palace and spend the night with her family, sharing with them the imperial dumplings. Today dumplings eaten at Chinese New Year commemorate Yuan Xiao's adventure.

Native American Calendar

Historians believe that noting dates and recognizing units of time varied greatly among the different Native North American groups. Unfortunately no detailed calendar or explanation of calendaric calculation exists, probably because many groups kept such knowledge secret. Possible exceptions could be Kiowa calendars drawn on animal skin and the carved or drawn wheels found mostly in the Southwest, which might have a lunar connection. However, it is known that days, months, and seasons were observed and often used in a vaguely abstract reference to years. For example, although the precise concept of a month or year did not exist for Native Americans, they would refer to something having happened many moons (months) or winters (in reference to years) ago. In other words, it appears that short- and long-term knowledge of time was not nearly as important to Native Americans as the change of seasons. Being able to anticipate when a new season was approaching meant that, for example, agrarian groups would know when to prepare to plant crops, and groups of the Great Plains would recognize when to get ready to follow the migration of the buffalo herds.

Right: *This is believed to be a rare example of a Kiowa calendar. By deciphering the symbols drawn on this animal skin, the Kiowa may have been able to anticipate the change of seasons.*

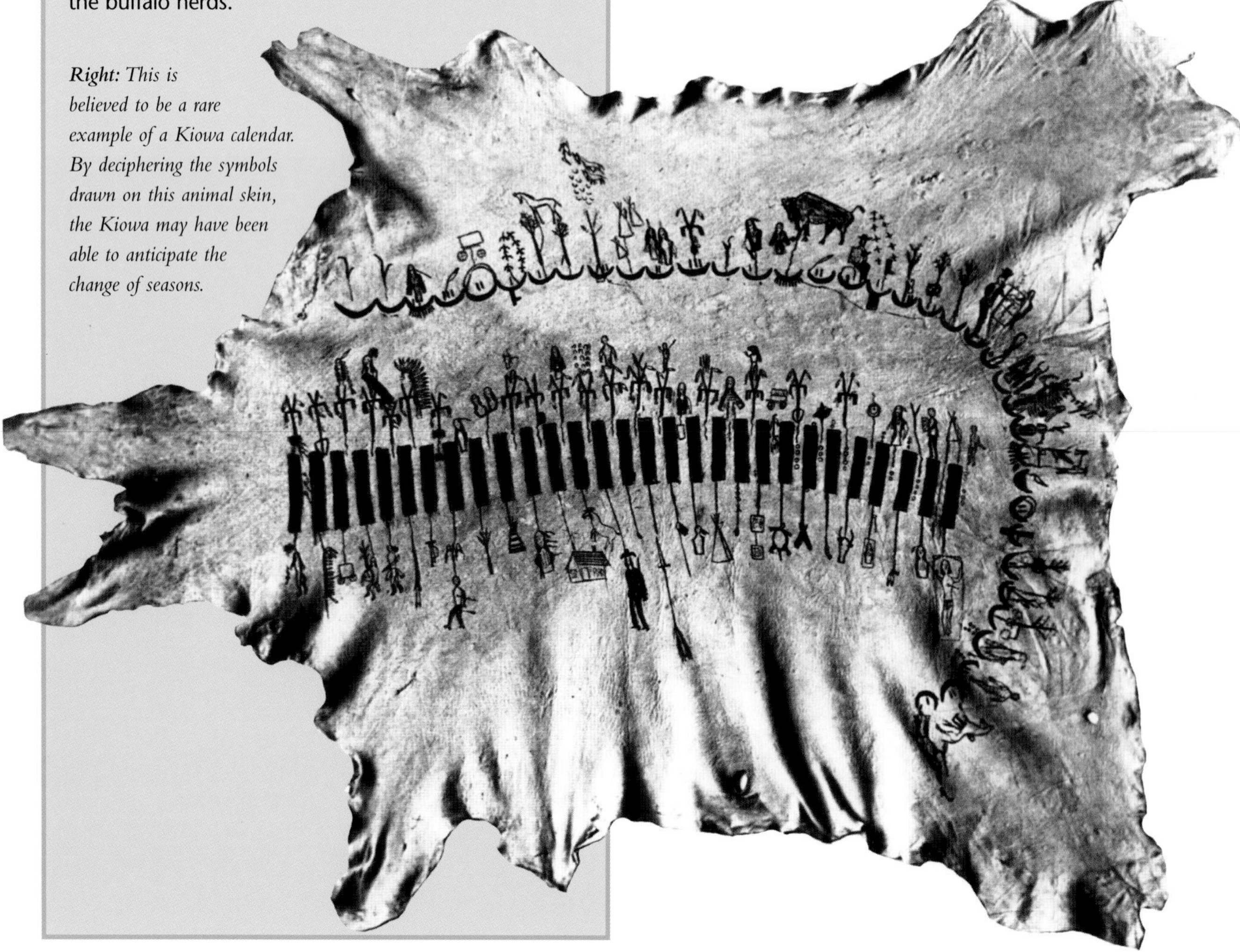

Vikram Samvat includes the new year celebration Diwali, also known as the Festival of Lights, and is still used to fix the dates of many special religious days.

The Yugabdha divided the earth's age into four yugas or epochs: Satya, Tretaa, Dwaapar, and the current age, Kali. Each yuga lasted for a different number of years, with Kali being the shortest. The length of days also varied. They were determined by the crossing of the moon of a certain position in relation to the sun in the night sky. This meant that the days ranged from 20 to 27 hours, depending on the time of year. *Tithis* form part of the Vedic calendar, which is explained in the *Panchanga*, an ancient Hindu text. It divides the solar year into 360 days and cites 12 lunar months of either 27 or 28 days. Before the *Panchanga*, some Hindu astronomers followed the lunar year and some the solar year, but eventually the two were calculated together.

Celtic calendar

Historians have a very difficult time determining the exact workings of much of Celtic civilization and mythology because the druids, who were the priests, leaders, and scholars of the Celts, never recorded their rituals and belief systems, relying instead on oral teachings. Much of what is now known about ancient Celts comes from either the writings of the Roman leader Julius Ceasar (100–44 BCE), who invaded Celtic lands; from censored myths transcribed by medieval monks; or from archaeological and anthropological speculation. What is clear is that many Celtic cultures in western Europe and the British Isles divided the year into two periods of six months each.

A feast marked the beginning of each period. Beltane was held in early May, and Samhain (or Samain) in late October–early November. Of the two feasts, Samhain appears to have been the start of the Celtic new year because it celebrated the start of long dark nights. According to one myth, in the days that led up to Samhain, Lugh, the god of light, was killed by Tanist, the god of mayhem. Tanist would rule the cold earth until the god of light returned in the spring. With the advent of Christianity, Samhain began to be called All-hallows Eve and, eventually, Halloween.

According to a Celtic poem "The Song of Amergin," the year was made up of 13 months with an extra day or days at the end. Archaeologists, however, discovered the remains of a bronze plate that indicated that the Celtic calendar might have worked within a 19-year cycle of 235 lunar months. Some scholars believe that the Celts used a combination of both calendaric methods.

Mayan calendar

Some historians have argued that the Mayan calendar, which calculates the solar (or tropical) year at 365.242036 days, is more accurate than our current calendar, which has precisely 365.2425 days. To achieve such accuracy and to keep track of important religious, ceremonial, and administrative days, the ancient Maya devised a calendaric system made up of three different ways of determining dates. These included the Long Count, Tzolkin, and Haab.

Left: This Mesoamerican solar calendar was based on the one used by the Maya.

The Long Count was a mathematical method of keeping track of each day since the beginning of Mayan time, which experts have estimated as having started in August 3114 BCE. The Tzolkin, which had a year of 260 days, was used primarily for religious dates. The basis of Tzolkin was a 13-day week, with each day given a number from 1 to 13, and a 20-day week, with each day given a different name. Examples of Tzolkin dates are 4 Ahau and 8 Muluc. Because the shortest unit in the Long Count system (uinal) is equal to 20 days, the Tzolkin and Long Count complemented each other. This meant that it was possible to determine the Tzolkin-named week based on the last digit of the Long Count. For instance, in the Long Count 12.18.16.2.6 the last digit, or uinal, is 6, which signifies the sixth Tzolkin week, known as Cimi.

The Haab dating method was used for administration and governmental purposes. It was made up of 18 named months of 20 days each, numbered 0 to 19. This method worked in much the same way that modern days and months are noted. In the Haab system, for example, the third day of the month of Zotz is written 3 Zotz. To complete the solar year, five days were added at the end of the Haab calendar to give 365 days. These five

Norse Days of the Week

The Norse calendar named days of the week for deities. The deities were identified with a letter of the runic alphabet used by Germanic peoples of northern Europe. Sunday, the letter *S,* was named for the sun and was also associated with the solar serpent. Monday, the letters *OE, G,* or *ON,* was known as Moon's Day, or Manidagar, and was also associated with emotions, wildlife, moon cycles, and tides. Tuesday, the letter *T,* was the day of the god Tyr and was also associated with Polaris, the Pole Star. Wednesday, the letter *O,* was for Odin, the chief god of the Old Norse pantheon, and all sites sacred to him. Originally associated with the fury of stormy nights, Odin was eventually seen as lawgiver, as lord of the runes and their magic power, and as the god of transformation. Thursday, the letter *TH,* was for the thunder god Thor. Friday, the letter *F,* was for Frigga, an earth-daughter and consort of Odin. She shared in Odin's wisdom, presided over marriages, and was invoked by women during childbirth. In one myth Frigga traveled through nine worlds in order to win eternal life for her son Balder, but he was slain by a dart made of mistletoe. His death was associated with the summer solstice. Finally Saturday, the letter *D,* was for the god Seater (possibly after the Roman god Saturnus), who was believed to signal beginnings and endings.

intercalated days, known as Uayeb, were thought to be unlucky and dangerous, and the Maya stayed home when they could and prayed.

To synchronize the Tzolkin and Haab dating systems, the Maya invented a calculation method known as the Calendar Round. This method brought the two dating systems together and tabulated each day precisely within a 52-year cycle. One theory for the purpose of the Maya's complex calendars is that they believed that ruling deities changed daily and influenced each day for good or evil. This meant that accurate timekeeping was necessary to tell which deity was in charge each day. The Maya calendar, minus the Long Count, was the basis of all subsequent Mesoamerican calendars, including that of the Aztecs.

Calendars of ancient Greece

The system for calibrating time in ancient Greece varied from city-state to city-state. For example, in Athens the new year started in summer, in Sparta it started in fall, and in Delos in winter. Although the Greeks were accomplished astronomers, their calendars appeared random. In 432 BCE a 19-year cycle, known as the Metonic cycle, was introduced. The Metonic cycle—named for the Athenian

Below: *A man butchers a boar in November in this Roman calendar mosaic, now located in Santa Maria del Popolo cathedral in Pavia, Italy.*

astronomer Meton who invented it—began with 12 years, each with 12 lunar months. The first 12 years were followed by seven years, each with 13 lunar months. In total one cycle had 235 lunar months, and of those, 110 months needed to have 29 days and 125 months 30 days so that the lunar months and solar years would match.

The Metonic system was not always recognized by those who ran the civil calendar. As a result the arbitrary nature of ancient Greek civil calendars makes it difficult for modern historians to pinpoint precise dates. In Athens, for example, the length of the civil year was determined by the indefinite tenure of the city's archon (chief magistrate), for whom the year was named. Within the civil year, however, there were fixed lengths of time for the office of other political positions (*prytanies*), and historians rely on these when citing dates.

FRANCISCVS

IN QVORVM

Above: The signature of Pope Gregory XIII appears at the bottom of this papal document ordering the reform of the Julian calendar in the late 16th century.

Roman, Julian, and Gregorian calendars

Initially the Roman calendar started at the vernal equinox, the day in spring when day and night are of equal length. It was a 10-month lunar calendar of four 31-day and six 30-day months. According to legend it was invented by Romulus, the mythical founder of Rome. The year lasted only 304 days, and about 61 days of winter did not fall within the calendar at all. During the reign of Numa Pompilius (c. 715–673 BCE), the second king of Rome, the calendar was reformed, reducing the 30-day months to 29 days and adding two months, one with 29 days and one with 28. This extended the calendar year to 355 days.

The calendar remained unchanged until Julius Caesar amended it. The changes made while Caesar was ruler of Rome became known as the Julian calendar. The changes included basing the calendar on a solar year of 365 and a quarter days. The year was divided into 12 months of either 30 or 31 days, except for February, which was given 28 days. Then, because most years had 365 days instead of 365 and a quarter days, a leap day (the intercalation of February 29) was added every four years to make up the difference.

For centuries the Julian calendar seemed to work well. However, because the length of the solar year is actually 11 minutes 42 seconds longer than what had been calculated in Caesar's time, by the mid-16th century the calendar was roughly 14 days behind the start of the natural seasons. To correct the mistake Pope Gregory XIII (who reigned 1572–1585) made two major changes. First he got rid of several days in 1582, and second he amended the implementation of February 29 so that it only occurred in century years that were divisible by 400 (for example, 1600 and 2000). February in all other century years (1800, 1900, and 2100) was left with 28 days. The Gregorian calendar, as the amended system is now known, also set January 1 as the first day of the new year. Today the Gregorian calendar is recognized by the vast majority of peoples in the world.

ALYS CAVINESS

Bibliography

Pennick, Nigel. *The Pagan Book of Days: A Guide to the Festivals, Traditions, and Sacred Days of the Year.* Rochester, VT: Inner Traditions Intl. Ltd., 1999.

SEE ALSO: Apocalypse Myths; Aztecs; Celts; China; Cycles; Dragons; Druids; Egypt; Festivals; Germanic Peoples; Greece; India; Maya; Mesopotamia; Moon; Native Americans; Stars; Sun.

CALLISTO

Callisto was one of the many sexual conquests of Zeus, king of the gods, and therefore one of many characters in Greek mythology who suffered the jealous anger of Hera, Zeus's wife and queen. Hera transformed Callisto into a bear, which according to legend is the Great Bear constellation seen in the night sky.

***Above:** This early diagram of the Great Bear constellation comes from an Arabic manuscript. The Greek myth of Callisto explains how the bear came to be in the sky.*

Callisto was either a nymph or the daughter of Lycaon, a powerful king of Pelasgia. Both he and his sons were well known for being ruthless and untrustworthy. One day Zeus disguised himself as a humble workman and visited Lycaon to investigate his behavior.

When Zeus arrived in Pelasgia, Lycaon made a human sacrifice on Zeus's altar and then offered his guests some of the sacrifice to eat. Zeus was so disgusted by this blasphemy that he hurled thunderbolts at Lycaon and his sons, killing them instantly. Other versions of the myth have it that Zeus killed the sons but turned Lycaon into a wolf. Zeus then ordered a huge flood (Deucalion's Flood) to inundate and cleanse the earth.

After the death of her father and brothers, Callisto sought refuge with Artemis (Diana in Rome), goddess of the hunt. Artemis was renowned for her chastity and her dislike of male company. She lived in the forest, where she hunted with a select band of young women who were all sworn to virginity and loyalty to the goddess.

Zeus saw Callisto asleep in the forest. He disguised himself as Artemis and succeeded in seducing Callisto, who became pregnant. Fearful of the consequences if her pregnancy should be discovered, Callisto succeeded in hiding her condition from Artemis and her companions for nearly nine months. One hot day, however, the band of huntresses went down to the stream to bathe. As the young women disrobed, Callisto could no longer hide her secret. The goddess was furious at Callisto's breach of the rules of virginity, and in spite of the girl's pleading, Artemis exiled Callisto from the band. One of the most famous depictions of the banishment of Callisto is a painting by the Venetian artist Titian (c. 1489–1576) entitled *Diana and Callisto*. Soon after the banishment Callisto, wandering alone in the forest, gave birth to a baby boy, whom she named Arcas.

Hera's revenge

Up until this point in the story, Hera had done nothing to punish Callisto. The birth of the baby, however, was too much for the queen of the gods to endure. Hera leaped on Callisto and threw her to the ground. Callisto, pleading with Hera to spare her, could only watch with horror as her own arms and legs grew hairy and rough and her nails grew long and pointed. Soon the transformation was complete. In her jealous anger Hera had turned Callisto into a bear.

Callisto fled deep into the Pelasgian forest and lived alone in despair. Because her mind remained human, she fully understood what had happened to her. Yet her bear's mouth would not allow her to talk, only growl, so she had no way of warning hunters that she was not to be feared.

Meanwhile, Zeus had given Arcas to one of his previous lovers, Maia, to raise. Maia was the eldest of the seven sisters who form the constellation of the Pleiades. In the past Zeus had seduced her too, and she had given birth to Hermes, messenger of the Olympian gods.

When Arcas was 15 he went into the Pelasgian forest to hunt. Callisto, who was still living in the forest, recognized her son immediately. She followed Arcas because she was curious to see him and longed to be near him, but she knew she had to stay hidden. Suddenly Arcas caught sight of the bear and pursued her.

Arcas was about to kill Callisto with his bow and arrow when Zeus intervened. He snatched up Callisto and set her into the heavens, so saving Arcas from the crime of killing his mother. The god transformed Callisto into a constellation, the Great Bear and Arcas into the brilliant star Arcturus. (According to another version of the myth, Arcas became king of Pelasgia as the heir of his grandfather Lycaon, and the land of Pelasgia was renamed Arcadia in his honor.)

Hera was not happy at seeing her one-time rival's sufferings cut short, especially by the intervention of her own husband. She went to see her old nurse Tethys, the wife of the ocean, Oceanus. Tethys sympathized with Hera. She forbade the new constellation ever to plunge into the ocean to drink, which is why the Great Bear constellation never sets into the ocean, as other stars do, but always remains above the horizon.

Callisto in the heavens

In astronomy the Great Bear, which was named for Callisto, is also known as Ursa Major (meaning "Great Bear" in Latin). It is a constellation that is often seen in the northern hemisphere and includes the Big Dipper, or Plow. Another astronomical reference to Callisto is the second largest satellite (moon) orbiting Jupiter. The moon, named Callisto, is nearly as large as the planet Mercury.

PETER CONNOR

Bibliography

Apollodorus, and Robin Hard, trans. *The Library of Greek Mythology.* New York: Oxford University Press, 1999.

Bulfinch, Thomas. *Bulfinch's Mythology.* New York: Modern Library, 1998.

Howatson, M. C., and Ian Chilvers. *Concise Oxford Companion to Classical Literature.* New York: Oxford University Press, 1993.

SEE ALSO: Artemis; Diana; Flood Myths; Hera; Lycaon; Nymphs; Oceanus; Pleiades; Stars; Virginity; Zeus.

Below: This 16th-century painting by Titian shows the moment when Artemis (Diana) banishes Callisto from her band of huntresses.

CALYPSO

Calypso was a nymph and goddess who lived on a remote island called Ogygia. She is famous for playing host to Odysseus during his journey home after the Trojan War. According to Homer's *Odyssey,* the Greek hero stayed with Calypso for seven years, during which time she tempted him with an offer of immortality. Odysseus's refusal to accept the offer reflected his love for his homeland of Ithaca and his wife, Penelope.

Above: *This 17th-century tapestry depicts Odysseus arriving at the island of Calypso, one of the many islands visited by the Greek hero during his 10-year journey home from the Trojan War. In the most widely known version of the myth, Odysseus arrived at the island alone.*

Different sources give various figures as the parents of Calypso. In the *Odyssey*, the epic poem by the Greek poet Homer (c. ninth–eighth century BCE), she is said to have been the daughter of Atlas, one of the Titans. Atlas was the father of a large number of daughters, many of whom, like himself, were associated with the sea and remote, otherworldly places. Other sources name other parents for Calypso, mostly associated with the sea, and the sea Titan, Oceanus, is usually said to be either a parent or grandparent. Calypso was thus a venerable and elemental figure. Calypso's name is derived from the Greek verb *kalyptein* and may mean "hider" or "concealer."

The *Odyssey* gives a full description of Calypso and the magical island of Ogygia on which she lived. Her home was a cave, warmed by a cedarwood fire. The cave was situated in a lush forest setting of alder, poplars, and cypress trees. Owls, hawks, and gulls nested there; clusters of grapes hung from a vine over the mouth of the cave; and clear water flowed from not one, but four fountains. Nearby, meadows bloomed with parsley and violets. Calypso lived on ambrosia and nectar—the food and drink of the gods. The goddess spent her days weaving, an activity associated with femininity and domesticity.

The arrival of Odysseus

Odysseus arrived at this island paradise as a solitary castaway, bereft of everything after several years of travel and arduous adventures. The one remaining ship of his fleet had been destroyed by a storm sent by the gods and all his men had been killed. For Odysseus, Calypso was a savior, like several other women encountered by him during his travels.

At first, Odysseus was very happy to be with Calypso, but gradually he spent more and more time sitting on the rocks by the seashore, looking out to sea and yearning for his homeland of Ithaca and his wife, Penelope. When Zeus finally sent Hermes, the messenger of the gods, with instructions for Calypso to release Odysseus, she did so, helping him build a raft to continue his journey. First, though, she tried to persuade him to stay, offering him immortality and the opportunity to spend the rest of time with her on Ogygia. Odysseus's refusal, and his insistence

Above: Ulysses and Calypso *by Italian painter Luca Giordano (1641–1711). The painting shows Calypso pouring from a pitcher and attended by handmaidens, although in Homer's* Odyssey *she lived alone.*

on remaining mortal and returning to Ithaca, is a significant symbolic moment in the sequence of tests and challenges that he faces on his long journey home.

Some scholars have proposed that Calypso symbolizes one of several variant forms of marriage offered to Odysseus as alternatives to his ideal of life with Penelope on Ithaca. Calypso represents a form of utopian isolation. Other women encountered by the hero on his travels offer different forms of romantic bliss. For example, the princess Nausicaa, whom Odysseus encountered when he was shipwrecked on the island of Scheria, represented the pleasures of family life.

Calypso's children

Several sons were said to have been born to Calypso and Odysseus. Two, Nausithous and Nausinoos, have names that reflect their nautical ancestry. Another mentioned by some sources is Latinus, who became the king of the Latins in Italy. Calypso was also said by some early sources to be mother of Telegonus, although others say his mother was the enchantress Circe. Telegonus later came to Ithaca and accidentally killed his father Odysseus.

Calypso rarely featured in ancient Greek art. However, from around 1600 CE the story of Odysseus and Calypso became popular with European painters. It was around this time that Flemish artist Jan Brueghel the Elder (1568–1625) painted *Fantastic Cave Landscape with Odysseus and Calypso*, which depicted Odysseus and Calypso sitting in a romantic embrace against a lush backdrop. Around 70 years later, Dutch artist Gerard de Lairesse painted the more dramatic *Hermes Ordering Calypso to Release Odysseus.* Another 17th-century artist, the Italian Luca Giordano, also depicted the pair. His *Ulysses and Calypso* (Ulysses was the Roman name for Odysseus) shows Calypso pouring a drink for her guest.

ANTHONY BULLOCH

Bibliography

Bulfinch, Thomas. *Bulfinch's Mythology.* New York: Modern Library, 1998.

Homer, and Robert Fagles, trans. *The Odyssey.* New York: Penguin USA, 1999.

SEE ALSO: Atlas; Circe; Hermes; Odysseus; Penelope; Zeus.

CANAAN AND PHOENICIA

The biblical promised land of the ancient Hebrews, Canaan covered parts of Palestine, Israel, and Jordan. The same area, as well as Lebanon, was later home to the Phoenicians. Many of the Phoenician myths and deities were inherited from the Canaanites, but as the Phoenicians spread throughout the Mediterranean, many of the city-states developed their own versions of the gods and myths.

The Canaanites were a collection of different peoples who occupied villages and towns in and around Palestine. These people shared a common language and followed similar religious beliefs. From around 1550 to 1200 BCE the Canaanites were ruled at one time or another by the Egyptians and the Hittites from Anatolia. Between 1400 and 1200 BCE the first writing system that included consonants was invented by the Canaanites in order to administer their extensive trade. It was a cuneiform (wedge-shaped impression) system with 31 distinct signs. The Canaanite script would later influence the Phoenician one, the 22 signs of which formed the basis for our present-day alphabet.

During the 12th century BCE much of the territory inhabited by the Canaanites was conquered by the Israelites and the Sea Peoples (possibly peoples from Crete). Because of the invasions, some Canaanites were forced to move to cities and villages along the Mediterranean coast in what is now modern Lebanon. Historians believe that these peoples became the Phoenicians.

There are two theories for the derivation of the name *Phoenicia*. The Greek word *phoinikes*, by which the Greeks called the

Below: This ancient gold pendant in the shape of a Phoenician boat reflects the importance of trading to the seafaring Phoenicians.

Phoenicians, refers to the purple dye that the Phoenicians produced and traded, which was highly valued in the Mediterranean world. The other theory says that the derivation comes from the Phoenician word *fenchu*, meaning "shipbuilder."

The Phoenicians' city-states were generally independent, with their own kings and small senates. Some of the largest and wealthiest Phoenician city-states included Byblos, Sidon, Tyre, and Ugarit. The Phoenicians were highly skilled merchants and sailors, and they built a lucrative network of Mediterranean coastal markets, including their most famous colonial city, Carthage (near modern Tunis), founded in the ninth century BCE. They also maintained an intense rivalry with the Greeks for control of the sea routes from their colonial markets. They traded in many products, such as linen, purple dye, craftworks, wine, oil, and slaves. Centuries later, Phoenicia was taken over successively by Assyria, Babylonia, Persia, and, in 332 BCE, Alexander the Great, until the Romans incorporated it into the province of Syria.

Canaanite gods

The religions of both the Canaanites and Phoenicians were polytheistic, with elements assimilated from neighboring cultures, including the Egyptian, Mesopotamian, and ancient Arabic worlds. The chief Canaanite deity was El, meaning "god." He was known as the supreme creator, father of gods, men, and time; he was omniscient, wise, and merciful. El had two wives, Asherah and Anat (also called Astarte). It was believed that the morning stars were the offspring of El and Asherah, and that El and Anat were the parents of the evening stars. El was usually depicted wearing a horned crown and sitting on a throne, receiving the homage of and bestowing blessings on the kings of Ugarit, an important city-state in Canaan located near the modern Syrian city of Ras Shamra.

One of El's sons—or grandsons, according to some versions—was Baal, god of fertility. Baal castrated and dethroned, depending on the version, either El or Dagon, who was sometimes referred to as Baal's father, and then married Asherah and Anat. Usurpation myths such as the story of Baal and El or Dagon may have influenced similar myths in other cultures, for example, that of Uranus and Cronus in ancient Greece. In one version of El's myth, following Baal's victory, the supreme creator took refuge in the primeval abyss, the ocean into which all the rivers flowed, and tried to recover his power with the aid of Yam (Sea). Yam was a female sea monster with seven heads who was similar to the Greek Poseidon.

Yam defeated Baal in their first battle, but then Baal joined forces with Anat, goddess of war and love, and together they defeated Yam. Baal's victory over Yam meant that he was the only deity with enough power to control the waters from the sky (rain). For the Canaanites the goddess Yam represented the chaotic and primeval ocean, and Baal symbolized the rain. One interpretation of the myth is allegorical, explaining why the sterile and salty water of the female sea monster Yam was always defeated by the fresh rainwater of the fertility deity Baal, which helped to bring life to the crops. Baal, also known in some parts of Canaan as the god of life, was representative of the cycle of death and resurrection as seen in both the change of seasons and the process of wilting and rebirth of vegetation and crops.

The myth of Baal and Yam is similar to an earlier one from Mesopotamia featuring Apzu and Tiamat, and also to an Egyptian one that deals with the heavenly conflict between Osiris-Isis and Seth. Baal also imitated Egyptian deities in terms of his appearance. He was usually represented brandishing a scepter or mace, while holding a tree-spear of life, like some Egyptian gods. He was also shown enthroned, wearing a horned crown and receiving gifts from his worshipers.

Canaanite and Phoenician Pantheon

Adonis: Canaanite and Phoenician agrarian god; later adopted by the Greeks.
Anat: One of El's consorts and the Canaanite goddess of love and war.
Asherah: One of El's consorts and the Canaanite goddess of craftsmanship.
Ashtar: In Canaanite mythology, Baal's son and one-time king of the sky.
Astarte: Also Ashtart or Ashtoreth; Phoenician goddess of fertility, Baal's consort, and in some places the chief deity.
Baal: God of the sky, rain, and fertility in both Canaanite and Phoenician mythology.
Baalat: Phoenician mother of the gods.
El: Supreme creator in Canaanite and Phoenician mythology.
Melqart: Also Melkart and Melkarth; Phoenician chief sun god and patron of ships and sailors.
Mot: Son of El and Canaanite god of death and the underworld.
Resheph: Canaanite god of plague and the underworld; Phoenician sun god, similar to the Greek Apollo.
Shapash: Canaanite sun goddess.
Yam: Canaanite female sea monster and goddess of the sea.

After Baal's victory, his former ally Anat turned on him and decided to kill his followers—the reasons for her actions are unknown. Then Baal attempted to get control over Anat, which he did by revealing to her the secret of making storms, thunder, and lightning. This is similar to the Egyptian myth of the Destruction of Mankind, where Sekhmet, a lion goddess, was sent by Re to destroy the race of men, but afterward she had to be tamed by Re himself. Another well-known parallel is the biblical myth of the Great Flood, also found in Sumerian and Babylonian cultures.

Baal versus Mot

In another myth Baal later complained that he was the only god without a palace and wanted to have his own. Anat intervened on his behalf with El, who finally gave Baal a palace where he could be worshiped, proclaiming his power to everyone. This was exactly the same thing that the Mesopotamian god Marduk did after defeating the monster Tiamat—in fact, Baal's temple in Ugarit was similar to Marduk's in Babylon. Then Baal wanted to test if there was anyone able to resist his power, and his brother Mot, god of death, accepted the challenge. Baal agreed to meet Mot in the underworld, taking his clouds and rain with him, but Mot killed Baal while he slept.

As a result of Baal's death, the sky was without a king. Asherah, or El in another version, designated Baal's son Ashtar as his successor, but Ashtar turned out to be an incompetent ruler. Meanwhile, El began to regret Baal's disappearance and feared for the survival of humankind, which was now endangered without its divine protector. Then Anat decided to help Baal. Depending on the version, she either killed Mot in a battle, tearing his body apart and burning and grinding the pieces, or Anat went to the underworld and, with the help of Shapash, the sun goddess, resurrected Baal, who returned to the sky as its king.

In one version of Mot's death, his ashes were scattered throughout the fields as fertilizer for the farmers' crops. For the Canaanites the meaning of this story was that every year after the summer's long drought under the rule of

***Right:** Tanit, represented here in an ancient Phoenician terra-cotta sculpture, was the main female deity for the Carthaginians.*

Mot, there was fertility in the fall when Baal returned to the earth. After the resurrection of Baal, the whole universe recognized Baal's supremacy, and he presided over an age of peace. Meanwhile Yam retained her authority over the sea, and Mot over the underworld.

__Above:__ The ruins of the Temple of Baalat (foreground) are all that remain of the shrine built to honor the main Phoenician deity of Byblos.

Phoenician gods

The Phoenician religion varied in individual cities. Sidon had a primeval god, also called Baal, whose partner was Astarte, the mother goddess of fertility and love. Astarte was the same goddess as the Sumerian Inanna, the Babylonian Isthar, and the Egyptian Isis. In western colonies she was called Tanit (or Tinith, Tinnit, and Tint). She was especially important in Carthage, where she was considered the chief goddess. Tanit had been worshiped there ever since the fifth century BCE, when she eclipsed the leading male deity, Baal Hammon (Amon). Although she seems to have had some connection with the heavens, she was also a mother goddess, and fertility symbols often accompanied representations of her. She was probably the consort of Baal Hammon and was often given the epithet "face of Baal." In the area of Carthage at least, she was frequently listed before him on monuments. Tanit was also worshiped on the islands of Malta and Sardinia and in Spain.

In the worship of Tanit and Baal Hammon, children, probably firstborns, were possibly sacrificed. Evidence of the practice has been found west of Carthage in the precinct of Tanit, named for the Phoenician deity, where a *tophet* (a sanctuary for the sacrifice of children) has been uncovered (see box, page 271).

Another god of Sidon was Eshmun, an underworld healing divinity, similar to the Greek god of healing, Asclepius (or Asklepios). In Byblos the original supreme divinity was El, but he was later replaced by Baalat (Lady), who represented cosmic fertility. Baalat was the mother of gods and the protectress of the kings of the city. The evidence for the myth of Baalat was found on stone stelas (engraved pillars) that had carvings of her accepting offerings and gifts. On the stelas Baalat was enthroned and depicted with the Egyptian features and gestures usually attributed to Isis or Hathor. There were also statuettes that showed her naked, covering her breasts with her hands.

Ancient Adonis and Melqart

Baalat's male partner was Adonis, or Adon, ("Lord"), a young fertility god. Adonis died and was resurrected every year, proclaiming to his devotees the hope for eternal life. He was adapted from the Sumerian Dumuzi and the Babylonian Tammuz. Later the god Adonis was assimilated into Greek mythology, where he became the lover of Aphrodite. In Thrace Zalmoxis was worshiped as a version of Adonis; the Greek god of wine Dionysus may have been related to him. The Phoenician Adonis, like Baal in Canaan and Persephone in Greece, represented the annual winter death of nature and its resurrection every spring.

In the Phoenician city-state of Tyre, the main deity was Melqart, also called Melkart or Melkarth and known as the king of the city. He was a god with solar characteristics and the patron of navigators. Every year festivals of spring and winter were celebrated at Melqart's temple in Tyre, and his cult was extended throughout the Mediterranean as the Phoenicians expanded overseas. He was represented as a bearded man with a high and rounded hat, and Egyptian influence can be seen in the ankh he usually held. When the merchants of Tyre wished to establish a colony, they offered sacrifices to Melqart, waiting for an augury. If the sign was favorable, they would build their trading station there; if it was unfavorable, they searched for another place.

Melqart's female partner was Astarte. The Greeks compared the pair to their own gods Heracles and Aphrodite. Melqart was also named Malku and equated to the Babylonian Nergal, god of earth and the underworld. Another divinity was Resheph, who was considered the inventor of the plow and the sowing of cereal crops. The Greeks identified Resheph with Apollo.

An important feast in Tyre commemorated Melqart's resurrection during the spring. The citizens of Tyre burned an image of the god, thinking that in this way they contributed to the resurrection of Tyre's founder. Then they celebrated the sacred marriage of Melqart and Astarte. In

Below: ***The remains of the Temple of the Obelisks, also called Baalat Gebal, in Byblos. The temple was one of the most famous Phoenician shrines in the entire ancient Mediterranean world.***

Human Sacrifice

Scholars disagree about the occurrence of human sacrifices, called *mold,* among the Phoenicians and later among the Carthaginians. Philon of Byblos and the early Christian theologian Eusebius of Caesarea (c. 260–340) thought they consisted of sacrifices of children burned in a sacred fire. The Greek writers Diodorus Siculus (first century BCE) and Plutarch (c. 46–120 CE) claimed that the children's immolation (sacrifice) took place in front of their parents in the *tophet*, a type of shrine or special enclosure. According to some researchers, in Carthage the firstborns were beheaded and then placed in the hands of a statue of Baal Hammon. Later their corpses were thrown into the sacred fire.

Historians believe that these gruesome rites were practiced in periods of danger, epidemic, or drought. Archaeologists have not been able to confirm the existence of *tophets* in Phoenicia, but Diodorus Siculus tells of the sacrifice of hundreds of firstborns of the aristocracy of Carthage in order to placate Baal Hammon's rage when the city was besieged by the Sicilian Greeks in 310 BCE. Other researchers deny that such instances of infanticide took place. They think that such rituals consisted simply of prayers and acts of purification in which Phoenician children were offered symbolically. Alternatively, animals, slaves, or prisoners could have been sacrificed instead. These rites may also have been practiced by taking advantage of the natural death of children or fetuses in order to obtain their spiritual resurrection.

Right: *This wall engraving from Carthage, made around the early fourth century BCE, depicts a priest holding an infant in his left arm. Some experts think that the infant, perhaps a firstborn, is being prepared for a ritual sacrifice.*

Byblos the Phoenicians celebrated the Adonias, festivals whose aim was the resurrection of Adonis. During the festival women shaved their heads, went weeping through the streets, and prostituted themselves, as Astarte, Adonis's lover, had done in a Phoenician myth. In acting this way, they hoped to resurrect the god and bring good harvests. At the end of the festival there was a funerary banquet during which they presented gifts of fruits and cereals.

Religious festivals and ceremonies

Temples and shrines were not just places of worship in Phoenician cities, they were also the center of social life. People worked there at various jobs, but mainly as priests, among whom the role of high priest was held by the king. In the temple there were prophets and clairvoyants, barbers, and musicians, but the best-known and strangest figures were the hierodules (temple slaves), priestesses devoted to Astarte. The hierodules practiced sacred prostitution by offering their bodies in the temple to the first man who wished to sleep with them. The purpose was to reenact and renew the sacred marriage of their gods and to promote good harvests, among other things, throughout the world.

The architecture of the Phoenician temples influenced the design of those in Israel. In particular, the Temple of Melqart in Tyre served as the model for Solomon's Temple in Jerusalem. The temples had a frontal portico with columns, an atrium, and the *sanctum sanctorum,* the inner sanctum or "holy of holies," where different kinds of stelas, monoliths, and statues of divinities were stored. Other famous Phoenician temples include the Baalat Gebal in Byblos, also known as the Temple of the Obelisks, and the Temple of Baal Shamem in Tyre. The tops of mountains were also considered sacred places because it was believed that deities would appear there just as they did in temples.

JUAN FRANCISCO JORDÁN MONTÉS

Bibliography

Cotterell, Arthur. *Oxford Dictionary of World Mythology.* Oxford: Oxford University Press, 1986.

Nakhai, Beth Alpert. *Archaeology and the Religions of Canaan and Israel.* Atlanta, GA: American Schools of Oriental Research, 2001.

Rosenberg, Donna. *World Mythology: An Anthology of the Great Myths and Epics.* New York: McGraw-Hill, 1994.

SEE ALSO: Adonis; Astarte; Baal; Creation Myths; Egypt; Fertility; Festivals; Flood Myths; Sacrifice; Sea.

CASSANDRA

Cassandra was the daughter of King Priam and Queen Hecuba of Troy. She was given the gift of seeing the future by the god Apollo. However, when she angered the god, he turned the blessing into a curse, decreeing that no one would ever believe her prophesies.

According to the most common version of the myth of Cassandra, Apollo first set eyes on the princess when she fell asleep in his temple. Cassandra was very beautiful, and the god immediately fell in love with her. In an attempt to seduce her, Apollo gave her the gift of prophecy. However, although Cassandra accepted the gift, she refused the god's advances. Apollo was outraged and decided to punish her. The god persuaded Cassandra to give him just a single kiss, during which he planted a curse in the young woman's mouth. Although Cassandra would be able to predict the future, nobody would ever believe her prophecies.

Most of Cassandra's prophecies concerned the Trojan War, the 10-year struggle between Troy and Greece prompted by the Trojan prince Paris's abduction of the Spartan queen Helen. Paris was Cassandra's younger brother, but when he was born she implored her father to kill the baby because she had a premonition that he would lead to the city's fall. Priam did not take his daughter's advice. Instead he ordered that Paris be taken into the wilderness and abandoned.

Paris and the war

Paris was first nurtured by a she-wolf and then raised by shepherds. As a young man he was chosen by the goddesses Aphrodite, Athena, and Hera to be the judge of a contest between them. Paris had to decide who was the most beautiful of the three goddesses. He chose Aphrodite, who had promised him the love of the world's most beautiful woman.

When Paris returned to Troy in disguise, Cassandra recognized him and he was welcomed back by his father, Priam. It was not long, though, before Paris decided to sail to Greece and visit the various kingdoms there. Cassandra warned that her brother's voyage would bring destruction on Troy, but no one believed her, and Paris set off on his travels. While in Sparta, a Greek kingdom, Paris seduced Helen, the wife of the Spartan king Menelaus, and

Right: In the late 19th century sculptor Max Klinger created this striking statue of Cassandra by using a combination of marble and alabaster. Her piercing eyes of amber suggest her visionary powers.

persuaded her to return with him to Troy. This abduction angered the Greeks, who raised an army to set sail for Troy. So began a war that would last 10 years.

It was at the end of this period that Cassandra made one of her most famous prophecies. In a last, desperate attempt to breach the walls of Troy, the Greeks made a hollow wooden horse and left it outside the gates of the besieged city. Believing the Greeks to have fled and the wooden horse to be an offering to Athena, the Trojans opened the gates and brought it into the city. In fact the horse was full of Greek soldiers. The only Trojans to foresee the danger were Cassandra and the priest and seer Laocoon. As the horse approached the city, Cassandra began to scream, warning her fellow Trojans of the gift's real nature. However, viewing her as a madwoman, they ignored her.

The following night the Greek soldiers climbed out of the horse and let the rest of the Greek army into Troy. They proceeded to sack the city, killing and raping its inhabitants. Cassandra fled to the temple of Athena, where she hid, clasping a wooden statue of the goddess of war and wisdom. There she was found by Ajax of Locris, who dragged her out of the temple. Accounts vary as to whether Cassandra was raped by Ajax or not. In any case she was then claimed as a prize by the Greek king Agamemnon.

Smell of death

Cassandra returned to Mycenae with Agamemnon. However, Agamemnon's wife, Clytemnestra, and her lover, Aegisthus, had been plotting to murder the Greek king. On arriving at Mycenae Agamemnon approached the palace,

Left: A French print, dating from 1730, of Cassandra warning the Trojans against accepting the gift of a wooden horse that the Greeks have left outside the walls. The print is from a series by Bernard Picart (1673–1733) illustrating scenes from ancient legends.

Right: *The decoration on this ancient Greek plate shows Clytemnestra killing Cassandra with an ax.*

where his wife had prepared a banquet welcoming him home. Cassandra refused to enter, claiming that she could smell blood. This was to prove to be Cassandra's last prophecy, as Clytemnestra killed both her husband and his new mistress with an ax.

Sources and variations

Cassandra appears in the *Illiad,* the Greek poet Homer's eighth-century-BCE account of the Trojan War, but in the epic poem she is described as Priam's most beautiful daughter, and there is no mention of her powers as a prophetess. Much of what is known about her is drawn from the *Aeneid,* a work by the Roman poet Virgil (70–19 BCE). Another important source is the play *Agamemnon* by the Greek playwright Aeschylus (525–456 BCE), which tells the story of Cassandra's fateful journey to Mycenae, including her murder. The figure of Cassandra also features in the work of much later writers. For example, she appears in one of William Shakespeare's plays, *Troilus and Cressida,* written in 1602.

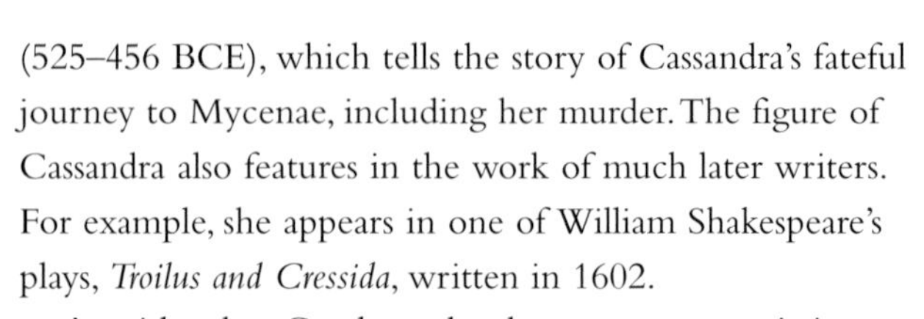

As with other Greek myths, there are many variations on the story of Cassandra. In one, as a young child she acquires the gift of prophecy after being left, along with her twin brother Helenus, in the Temple of Apollo. In this version the two children are attacked by the sacred serpents of Apollo, after which they both acquire the gift of prophecy. However, one of the key elements of the myth is removed—the idea that Cassandra brought her misfortune upon herself by angering the gods.

ANDREW CAMPBELL

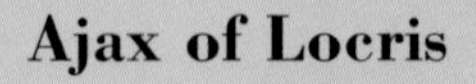

Ajax of Locris

Ajax of Locris was sometimes known as Little Ajax or Ajax the Lesser to distinguish him from the huge Ajax of Salamis, who fought the Greek prince Hector, Cassandra's brother, in single combat. Little Ajax was known for his speed as a runner and for the tame serpent that he carried with him. His abduction of Cassandra brought him the enmity of his fellow Greek heroes, who believed that he had aroused the hatred of Athena by violating the sanctity of her temple. Odysseus called for Ajax to be stoned, but he was allowed to sail home to Greece.

On the way home Ajax's ship was wrecked on the Gyraean Rock. Ajax managed to swim to safety, but when he boasted of his escape he was killed by Poseidon for his vanity. In one version of the myth, however, it was the wronged goddess Athena who killed him. Because Ajax had not atoned for his crime against Athena, the inhabitants of Locris were forced to appease the goddess themselves. The Delphic oracle told the Locrians to send two girls to Troy every year for a thousand years. Each pair would serve in the temple of Athena for a year before being replaced.

Bibliography

Homer, and Robert Fagles, trans. *The Iliad.* New York: Penguin USA, 2003.

Virgil, and Robert Fitzgerald, trans. *The Aeneid.* New York: Vintage, 1990.

SEE ALSO: Agamemnon; Aphrodite; Apollo; Athena, Clytemnestra; Greece; Hecuba; Helen; Laocoon; Paris; Priam.

CASTOR AND POLLUX

In both Greek and Roman myth the twins Castor and Pollux were seen as symbols of ideal brotherhood. Although one was mortal and the other divine, in death they were united as the constellation Gemini.

Known as the Dioscuri (literally "sons of Zeus"), Castor and Pollux (Roman)—or Polydeuces (Greek)—were thought of in classical mythology as twins, even though they had different fathers. They featured or took part in several key Greek stories, all of which occurred before the Trojan War. In addition the Roman Castor and Pollux fought alongside Roman soldiers in an early battle.

The conception of the twins occurred one night when Zeus (or Jupiter for the Romans) disguised himself as a swan and raped Leda, a mortal. That same night Tyndareos, king of Sparta and Leda's husband, made love to his wife. From Zeus's seed Leda gave birth to Pollux, while Castor was Tyndareos's offspring. According to another version that night Leda produced two eggs, one (fertilized by Zeus) containing Pollux and Helen, the other (by Tyndareos) forming Castor and Clytemnestra.

One of the Dioscuri's earliest adventures concerned their sister Helen. Before Helen was abducted by Paris, she was stolen by the Greek hero Theseus. Son of Aegeus and Aethra, Theseus was perhaps most famous for slaying the Minotaur. Several myths, including the one of the Minotaur, show Theseus treating women badly. The same was true of his abduction of Helen. She was rescued, however, by her brothers, who captured Theseus's mother, making her Helen's slave, a role she maintained until the fall of Troy.

Further adventures of the twins

The twins also sailed with the hero Jason on the *Argo,* and during the voyage Pollux killed the evil king Amycus in a boxing match. During their adventures at sea, Poseidon, according to one version, made the twins protectors of sailors and calmers of storms and waves. Greek sailors would later pray to the twins for safe voyages. It was also thought that Castor and Pollux appeared as part of the

Below: *Twelfth-century statues of the Dioscuri flank the entrance to Piabba del Campidoglio, Rome, designed by Michelangelo in the 16th century.*

Right: *This 17th-century painting by Peter Paul Rubens, a Flemish artist, depicts Castor and Pollux abducting the daughters of Leucippus, Pheobe and Hilaeira.*

natural phenomenon now known as Saint Elmo's fire, a luminous electrical discharge that is usually seen by sailors or from an aircraft during storms.

After their adventures with the Argonauts, the Dioscuri, along with other Greek heroes, took part in the legendary Calydonian boar hunt. They then returned to their native Sparta, where they abducted and raped (some versions say married) two women. Pheobe and Hilaeira were the daughters of Leucippus, and to avenge the rapes, Leucippus's nephews, Idas and Lynceus, attacked and killed Castor, the mortal twin. Another version has it that the fight between the Dioscuri and Idas and Lynceus (also known as the Messenian brothers) occurred over a disputed apportionment of stolen cattle. The Messenians had tricked the Dioscuri out of their fair share of the beef, and a fight ensued. Idas, who had earlier battled Apollo, killed Castor. Then Pollux killed Lynceus but was wounded in the head by Idas, who was in turn killed by Zeus.

Pollux was so grief-stricken at Castor's death that he pleaded with Zeus for Castor to be made immortal. As a compromise, Zeus allowed the twins to remain together on condition that they alternate days between living on Mount Olympus and in the underworld. Another version tells that Zeus transformed Castor and Pollux into the constellation Gemini.

Aiding the Romans

The Romans adopted the Dioscuri and added a significant legend. Around 500 BCE, troops of the new Roman republic fought the army of the deposed king, Tarquinius Superbus, at the Battle of Lake Regillus. The twins were seen either around the time of the battle watering their horses in the Forum, or fighting alongside the Roman soldiers on the battlefield. To honor the twins, a temple was dedicated to them in the Forum, and they appeared on Roman coinage. They also had their own secret cult.

CARL RUCK

Bibliography

Graves, Robert. *The Greek Myths*. New York: Penguin USA, 1993.

Howatson, M. C.,and Ian Chilvers. *Concise Oxford Companion to Classical Literature*. New York: Oxford University Press, 1993.

SEE ALSO: Helen; Jason; Leda; Rome; Theseus; Zeus.

CELTS

The Celts, who lived mostly in western Europe and the British Isles, were renowned warriors and craftspeople. Their religious practices and myths were overseen by priests called druids.

The Celts are disparate groups of mainly western European peoples who for many centuries have been mostly concentrated in the British Isles—especially Ireland, Wales, Scotland, and Cornwall—and in northern France. These people are linked by their dialects, which come from the Celtic language group, a branch of the Indo-European family of languages. As such, Celtic mythology resembles other Indo-European mythologies, especially Roman and Germanic mythologies.

Historians believe that the Celtic language group began to form between 1300 and 800 BCE. Despite the Celts' reputation as warlike peoples, current research suggests that the Celtic languages first spread through Europe not by conquest but through trade. The surviving Celtic languages are the Goidelic group, which includes Irish, Scottish Gaelic, and Manx, and the Brythonic group, which is made up of Welsh, Cornish, and Breton, the language of Brittany.

The earliest Celtic material culture is today known as the Hallstatt. It emerged in the region of southern Bavaria and Austria around 750 BCE. The wealth of this culture came from trade in Alpine salt and in iron, which was used for making weapons and utensils. Hallstatt culture was organized around a warrior aristocracy supported by craftspeople and farmers. Eventually the culture spread eastward into the Balkans and southwestward into France and northern Spain.

La Tène culture

Around 450 BCE the center of the Celtic world shifted to western Europe. This marked the beginning of La Tène culture, named for a site at Lake Neuchâtel in Switzerland. La Tène culture was more belligerent than the Hallstatt, but it also produced distinctive arts and crafts. The image most people have of Celtic art, with its elaborate images of animals and plants, is La Tène art.

Around 400 BCE, small groups of Celts began migrating outward from the core Celtic lands, probably as the result of overcrowding. To the south they encountered the Romans and even sacked Rome in the early fourth century BCE. To the southeast the Celts met the Greeks;

Left: The Celts were highly skilled metalworkers, as shown by this fourth-century-BCE bronze shield. The shield was found in London near Battersea Bridge and is now known as the Battersea Shield.

they attacked the temple of the oracle at Delphi in 279 BCE. Eventually a tribe known as the Galatians settled in Asia Minor (modern Turkey), but retained their Celtic language and culture. Around 370 CE, Saint Jerome, an early leader of the Catholic church, noted the similarity of the Galatian language to that spoken in Gaul (France). The Celts also migrated east and northeast from the Balkans to the Hungarian Plain and southern Poland. To the west they moved into the British Isles.

The Celts were never unified and did not form a centralized government or empire. They were not a nation or state, but a diffuse collection of peoples or clans who shared a common language group, material culture, and some myths. Celtic society only changed from a tribal to urban organization shortly before the Celts were conquered by the Romans in the first centuries BCE and CE. During that period Roman forces gradually subsumed Celtic groups one by one. In some places, such as Gaul (France) and southern Britain, Celts became Romanized fairly quickly, but in other places they retained their native culture beneath a veneer of Romanization, as in northern and western Britain. Ireland, however, remained almost completely outside the Roman world, except for trade relations. In Gaul and Britain a blend of Celtic and Roman cultures emerged, seen especially in the association of Celtic and Roman gods at sanctuaries and in temples.

Celtic religion

The Celts were polytheists, worshiping many gods. However, unlike Greek and Roman gods, who were associated with concepts such as love, wisdom, war, and hunting, Celtic deities were also associated with specific places and natural phenomena. The names of more than 400 Celtic gods have been identified from ancient inscriptions, but 300 of these names occur only once. Therefore scholars tend to think of Celtic gods in terms of general types rather than specific, named deities.

As a general rule Celtic deities were paired together; for example, a god of a tribe would be married to a goddess of the land. A typical pair was Sucellus (also known as the

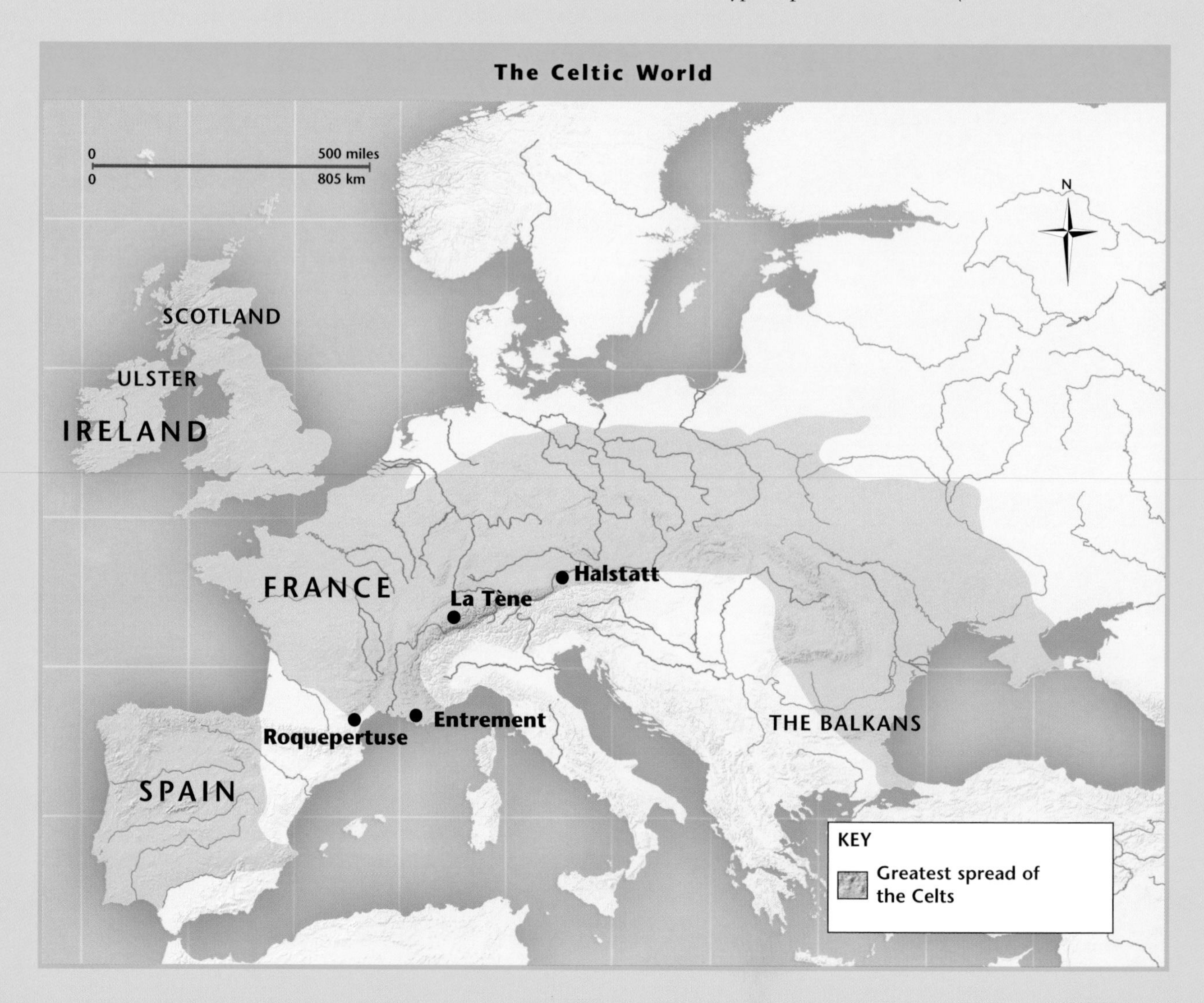

Some Celtic Gods

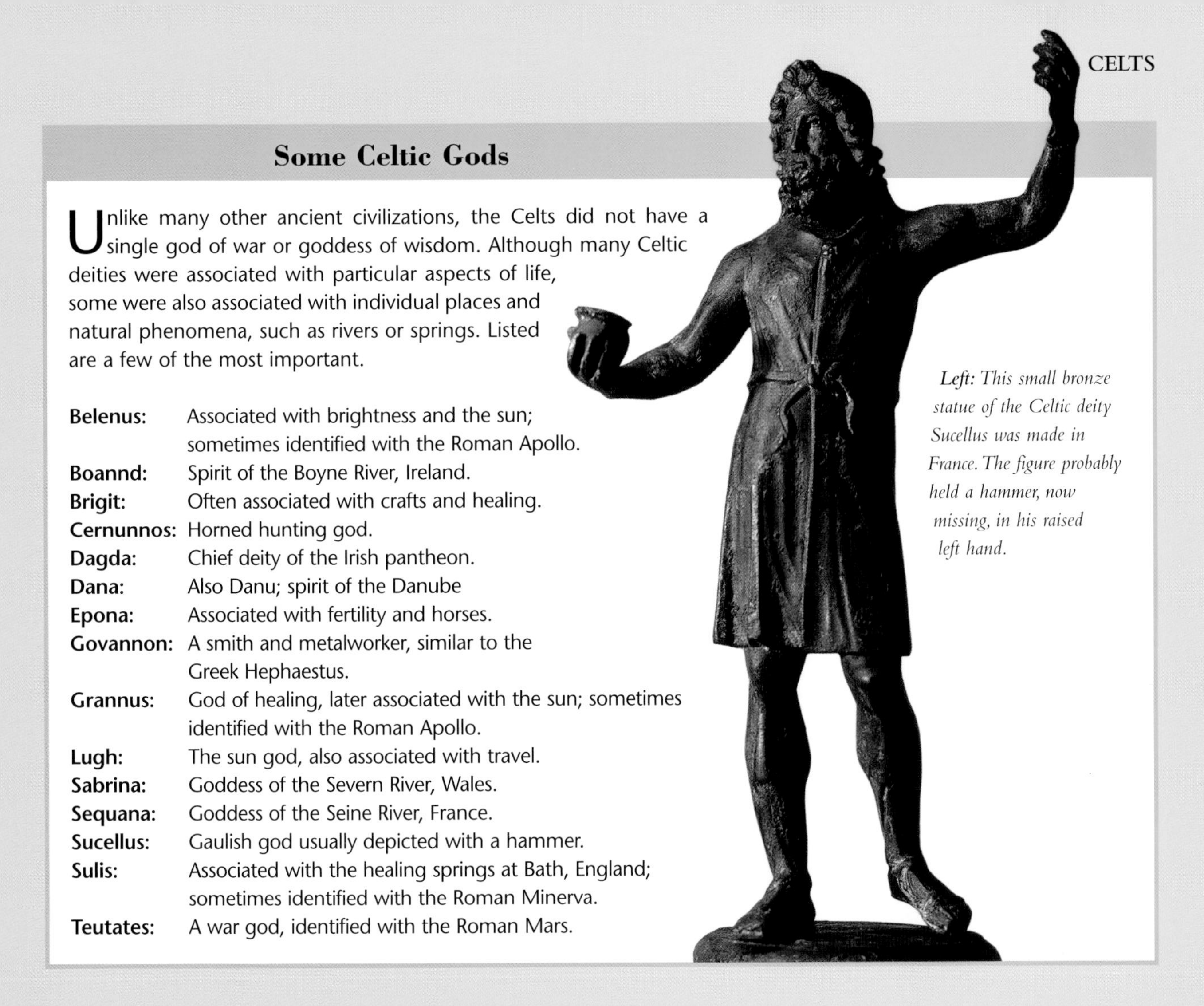

Unlike many other ancient civilizations, the Celts did not have a single god of war or goddess of wisdom. Although many Celtic deities were associated with particular aspects of life, some were also associated with individual places and natural phenomena, such as rivers or springs. Listed are a few of the most important.

Belenus: Associated with brightness and the sun; sometimes identified with the Roman Apollo.
Boannd: Spirit of the Boyne River, Ireland.
Brigit: Often associated with crafts and healing.
Cernunnos: Horned hunting god.
Dagda: Chief deity of the Irish pantheon.
Dana: Also Danu; spirit of the Danube
Epona: Associated with fertility and horses.
Govannon: A smith and metalworker, similar to the Greek Hephaestus.
Grannus: God of healing, later associated with the sun; sometimes identified with the Roman Apollo.
Lugh: The sun god, also associated with travel.
Sabrina: Goddess of the Severn River, Wales.
Sequana: Goddess of the Seine River, France.
Sucellus: Gaulish god usually depicted with a hammer.
Sulis: Associated with the healing springs at Bath, England; sometimes identified with the Roman Minerva.
Teutates: A war god, identified with the Roman Mars.

Left: This small bronze statue of the Celtic deity Sucellus was made in France. The figure probably held a hammer, now missing, in his raised left hand.

Good Striker, perhaps a thunder-and-lightning deity similar to Zeus and Jupiter) and Nantosuelta (the Winding River). As the Romans conquered the Celtic tribes, they often sealed their relationship with the Celts by marrying a local goddess to a Roman god, such as the Celtic Rosmerta (the Great Provider) and the Roman Mercury. Sometimes the Romans joined the name of a Roman male god with a Celtic male god, as in Apollo Grannus. Grannus was the Celtic god of healing and mineral springs such as those at Grand in Vosges, France. There was also a rare instance of a Celtic goddess who was merged with a Roman goddess, Sulis Minerva. This hybrid goddess was the deity of the mineral hot springs in Bath, England.

Celtic goddesses

Celtic goddesses were often the spirits of rivers and other bodies of water. Many of Europe's rivers were named for Celtic goddesses, such as the Seine (Sequana) in France, the Severn (Sabrina) in Wales, the Boyne (Boannd) in Ireland, and the Danube (Dana or Danu) in Germany and southeast Europe. The goddess Coventina was associated with a well in Carrowbaugh, along Hadrian's Wall in northern England.

The Dea Matres or Matronae (the Mothers) were a group of Celtic goddesses who were depicted as three seated women with symbols of fertility such as grain, fruit, bread, and babies. They were often accompanied by hooded dwarves known as Genii Cucullati (Hooded Spirits), who are thought to represent the fertility of the earth. A related goddess was Epona. She was depicted as a woman with a horse and a basket of fruit or grain. Epona's mare was often accompanied by a foal who was either suckling from the mare or being fed by Epona, also symbolizing fertility. Yet Epona was often also joined by a dog, representing both death and healing, or a raven, the sign of death in battle. Sometimes Epona carried a key, which has been interpreted as the key to the otherworld, the Celtic place of the afterlife. Epona, therefore, seems to stand for both life and death, war and healing.

Other Celtic goddesses included Rhiannon and Macha. In medieval Welsh mythology, Epona appeared as the goddess Rhiannon (Divine Queen). When Rhiannon was first seen by her future husband, she was riding a horse, like Epona. When she gave birth to a son, he was stolen from her and dead puppies left in his place. The boy was later found by a man named Teyrnon (Divine Prince) in a horse manger, in place of the mare's stolen foal. Rhiannon was punished for her son's disappearance by being forced to act like a horse and carry riders on her back. However, while she lived in the kingdom of Dyfed, the land was fertile and fruitful. Most of the imagery associated with Epona is also strongly associated with Rhiannon.

Machas in Irish mythology

Several beings named Macha appear in Irish mythology. One was a woman who appeared mysteriously in a widower's house and became his wife on the condition that he never speak of her to anyone. One day her husband went to a fair where he saw the king's horses racing. Without thinking, he exclaimed that his wife could run faster. The king forced him to bring Macha to race against the horses, even though she was pregnant. Macha won the race but went into labor as she crossed the finish line. She died in childbirth, cursing the men of Ulster (Northern Ireland) to be as weak as a woman in labor whenever they were in the most danger. Another Macha was one of the three goddesses of war. Her companion was named Badbh and often appeared in the form of a raven or crow. In this example, the two sides of Macha were split into two separate figures, one of fertility and horses, the other of death and black crows.

Lugh

The closest thing to a pan-Celtic god was Lugh (pronounced "loog"), to whom there were many dedications. Lugh appeared in medieval Irish and Welsh mythology as Lugh Samildánach (which means "Lugh, equally skilled in all arts") and Lleu Llaw Gyffes ("Lleu of the skillful hand"). The name Lugh may have had two meanings: one was "shining," linking him to the idea of a sun god; the other was "raven," connecting him to the Celtic war deities.

Lugh was also associated with shoes. An inscription to the "Lugoves" (Lugs) at Uxama in Spain was a dedication offered by a guild of shoemakers. For the Welsh, Lleu was one of the "three golden shoemakers of the Island of Britain," and in the *Mabinogi* (also *Mabinogion*), medieval tales of Welsh myths, he was disguised as a shoemaker when he received his nickname "skillful hand." The god's association with shoes suggests that he was considered to be a traveler, and this was one of the reasons for connecting him with Roman Mercury, the god of travel and trade. Celts of the Roman era were often buried with a pair of new shoes. This may indicate that the Celts believed that Lugh, as both the shoe god and the god of the dead, led the souls of the dead on their final journey.

Left: This statue is thought to be of Epona, the Celtic horse and fertility goddess. The statue comes from the Roman Forum at Alise Sainte Reine, France.

Roman interpretations

The Roman leader Julius Caesar (100–44 BCE) wrote about the Celts in *The Gallic Wars* (52–51 BCE), claiming that they worshiped Jupiter, Mercury, Mars, Minerva, and Apollo, and that they believed they were descended from Pluto or Dis, the Roman god of the underworld. This is a case of the *interpretatio romana*, in which Roman writers gave foreign deities names that would be more familiar to their readers. By Jupiter, Caesar probably meant the various striking gods, who were usually depicted holding hammers or clubs. Mercury was probably the god Lug, one of the most widely worshiped gods in the Celtic world (see box, opposite). Mars would have been the god of the tribe, who often seemed to be as much a healer as a warrior. His warlike qualities were used to protect his people. Apollo would have been one of the many healing gods. Minerva was harder to associate with a Celtic goddess, and Caesar may have meant a goddess like Brigit, who was associated with crafts and healing but was also linked to war. Pluto or Dis was probably one of the many Celtic gods of the dead and of the otherworld, many of whom had names meaning "dark" or "black."

The Roman poet Lucan, who lived in the first century CE, wrote that the Celts had three primary gods: Esus, Teutates, and Taranis. The name Esus had a meaning close to "lord" or "good master," Teutates meant "god of the tribe," and Taranis meant "thunderer." Each of these gods had a form of human sacrifice that was particular to him (see box, page 283): stabbing and hanging were the traditional ways of making offerings to Esus; sacrifices to Teutates were drowned; while worshipers of Taranis burned their victims. Medieval Celtic literature often depicted a triple death in which a king died by being stabbed and falling into a vat of liquid in a burning house, perhaps in a reference to the days when victims were sacrificed to all three of these gods.

The Cult of the Severed Head

Greek and Roman writers commented that the Celts were headhunters, taking their enemies' heads as trophies in war. The Celtic sanctuaries at Entremont and Roquepertuse in southern France display both depictions of piles of severed heads and actual skulls. Damage to the skulls shows that some of them were certainly taken in battle. Celtic warriors preserved the heads of their enemies by embalming them in cedar oil, bringing them out to display to visitors.

The head was believed by the Celts to be the seat of the soul, spirit, or intelligence, and severing the head was thought to concentrate these qualities by confining them to the skull. Medieval Welsh and Irish tales often featured severed heads that continued to speak after being detached from the body. The head of the mythical Welsh king Bran the Blessed (also known as Bendigeid Vran), son of the god Llyr, remained alive for 80 years after his decapitation, and was finally buried in London to protect the country from invaders. Irish tales tell of warriors mixing their enemies' brains with lime to form concrete-like brain-balls, which were exhibited as trophies. There are also tales of severed heads being kept in wells because it was believed that they magically affected the water, empowering the drinker with greater physical strength. Recent archaeological discoveries provide evidence for the practice of depositing heads in wells.

Right: *This ancient Celtic stone carving shows a mythical monster holding the severed heads of two men. Severed heads were highly prized by the ancient Celts.*

Above: *This early 20th-century illustration depicts Macha cursing the men of Ulster (Northern Ireland). According to legend, her curse on these men was that they would lose their strength in dangerous situations, such as fierce battles. Macha died in childbirth after competing in a race while pregnant.*

The otherworld

One of the popular themes of Celtic mythology was the journey to the otherworld. The Celts believed in life after death and buried food, weapons, and artifacts with the dead. The Celtic otherworld, to which the dead journeyed, was a place that almost coexisted with the mortal realm. The otherworld was known, depending on the region, as the Land of the Living, Land of the Young, or Delightful Plain, and according to the Romans was similar to Elysium, the Greek paradise where heroes dwelled after their deaths. It was a place where a soul would be happy and content forever. Time moved quickly—a hundred years in the living world lasted only a single day in the otherworld.

In the Celtic belief system a person might come across the otherworld by accident, for example, when the walls between the living world and the otherworld became thin. This could occur at certain times of the year, such as the festivals of Samhain (October 31 and November 1), or at specific places, such as fairy mounds, the far side of a fog bank, or places located "betwixt and between," such as boundaries, doorways, riverbanks, or wildernesses.

The otherworld was a place that could be amazingly luxurious and magical, but in some myths it could also be a place that was dark, grim, and often violent. The hero who journeyed there often assisted the inhabitants of the otherworld in some way. Sometimes he returned to his own world to find that everyone he knew had long been dead, because time moved so much faster in the otherworld. At other times he might return with something good to help his people, such as an object or some new knowledge or insight.

Another common theme of Celtic myths was one in which the king married a goddess known as Sovereignty, probably a reflection of the belief in the marriage of the

Human Sacrifice as Performed by the Celts

Human sacrifice among the Celts has long been a matter of controversy among historians. The classical writers who offer the most evidence for it are also the ones who seem to have had the most to gain by presenting the Celts as having performed the ritual. For instance, the suppression of the druids was justified by the accusation that they practiced human sacrifice, but the Romans may have been more interested in suppressing them because the druids encouraged rebellion against Rome. Julius Caesar claimed that the druids performed sacrifice by burning criminals in large wicker cages, while Diodorus Siculus (c. 90–21 BCE), a historian from Sicily, referred to druids stabbing their victims and taking divinations from their death throes. The Roman poet Lucan (39–65 CE) wrote that the gods each had their favorite forms of sacrifice, usually stabbing, burning, or drowning.

The clearest archaeological evidence for Celtic human sacrifice is a preserved body called Lindow Man for the place of his discovery in Cheshire, England. Believed to have died in his late 20s, Lindow Man was hit twice on the head, strangled, and stabbed in the throat before being deposited in a bog; bogs were believed to be sacred places. The bog preserved his body almost perfectly, from his death in the first century CE. until its discovery in 1983. The ritual manner of the murder suggests to archaeologists that he was a sacrifice. The lack of scars and muscular development on the body that would be associated with a life as a warrior or farmer suggests that Lindow Man may have been a druid himself.

Right: *This illustration is based on the idea that the Celts built giant wicker men and stuffed them with sacrificial victims before burning.*

Cernunnos

The god Cernunnos was often depicted as a seated man with horns or antlers growing out of his head. He was usually accompanied by a ram-horned snake and held a torque, a type of necklace that indicated high social status among the Celts. He is also depicted with bags of coins and grain, symbols of fertility and wealth. He seems to have been a type of deity known as the Master of the Animals, who controlled wild beasts and was probably appeased in some way in order to have a good hunt. Cernunnos's antlers linked him to stags, which were both the most important game animal to the Celts and, in mythology, the animals most likely to lead the unwary hunter into the otherworld. Cernunnos, like many mythic creatures that were part animal and part human, was an ambiguous deity, sometimes aiding humans but at other times placing them in danger.

Below: This lithograph is based on a stone carving from the first century BCE and shows the head of the god Cernunnos.

god of the tribe (represented by the king) and the goddess of the land. If the king was the true king, beloved of Sovereignty, the land would be fruitful, but if she turned against him, it was ravaged by war, famine, and plague.

Druids

The priests of the pagan Celts were known as druids. They were responsible for carrying out sacrifices, preserving mythology and history, advising the king, judging criminal cases and disputes, studying the natural world, and educating the children of nobles. Becoming a druid required as much as 20 years of study, and all knowledge was passed on orally to the next generation. The druids used the Greek alphabet for keeping financial accounts and other secular matters. However, religious material could not be written down and instead had to be memorized. This is one reason why so little is known for certain about pagan Celtic religion and mythology. Some scholars believe that the druids' most important duty was to perform sacrifices. These not only appeased the gods and encouraged them to favor the group with wealth and good fortune, but they were also used for divination of the future.

Because of the druids' wide range of responsibilities, religion was very important in Celtic society. The religious yearly calendar was divided into four parts, each beginning with a festival. The Irish names of the major festivals were Samhain (October 31 and November 1), Imbolc (February 1), Beltane (May 1), and Lughnasadh (August 1). This pattern is found in the Coligny calendar, dating from the first century BCE in France, as well as in Welsh and Irish medieval literature and modern folklore.

One of the roles ascribed to the druids was the ability to ban someone from participating in religious rites, thereby ostracizing him from the community. This was the worst possible fate for a Celt. The druids also taught that, after death, the soul was reborn either in this world or in the otherworld, a concept known as the transmigration of the soul. This belief was held so strongly that Celts would make loans to each other to be repaid in the next life, but it waned as Christianity became the dominant belief.

Early Christian influence

As Celts living in mainland Europe gradually became more assimilated into Roman culture, many began honoring Roman gods along with traditional Celtic ones. Some Romans deities thus acquired aspects of the Celtic gods. The Romans, meanwhile, tended to believe that it was best to worship as many gods as possible, so their pantheon continually expanded. The early Christian church had a very different view.

Christianity was legitimized in Rome by the emperor Constantine the Great in the early fourth century CE. By the fifth century the religion had spread into the British Isles and among Celtic groups. Over the course of the first millennium CE, traditional Celtic religious practices were gradually suppressed. However, many aspects of Celtic religion lived on in new forms as they were assimilated into Christianity. Saint Patrick, for example, seems to have taken over many aspects of the Celtic god Lugh (see box, page 280). Some historians believe that Saint Brigit was a pagan goddess adopted by the Christians.

Many Christian celebrations were based on Celtic festivals. One of the most famous is Halloween. It came from Samhain, which usually began on the evening of October 31. The ancient Celts celebrated Samhain as the end of summer. It marked the return of herds of livestock from the grazing pastures and the beginning of the Celtic new year. Before the festival large bonfires were erected on hilltops. These were set alight on October 31 in order to keep away both evil spirits and the unwelcome souls of the dead. It was believed that during the change from the end of one year to the beginning of a new one, lost souls would visit their former earthly homes. There were also demons, evil fairies, and other ghostly creatures of the night that would prey on mortals. At the same time, however, the Celts believed that Samhain was a good time for people to marry.

The sources of information about Celtic religion are very fragmented. There are no written sources that come directly from pre-Christian Celts themselves. Ancient Greek and Roman writers from the fifth century BCE to the second century CE, such as Herodotus, Posidonius, Diodorus Siculus, Strabo, Livy, and Tacitus, all wrote about Celtic religion, but their accounts were often biased according to whether they wished to emphasize how barbaric the Celts were or to criticize either Greek or Roman culture. Archaeological evidence provides imagery of gods and evidence of their worship, but without

***Right:** Saint Patrick, the patron saint of Ireland who converted the Irish Celts to Christianity, is depicted on the left in this 13th-century illustration. Jesus watches over the saint while he and the animals sleep.*

Animals in Celtic Mythology

The line between human and animal form was very indistinct in Celtic mythology. Some images of gods showed a humanlike figure accompanied by an animal, while others showed the deity as part human and part animal, either like the Greek Pan, who was half human and half goat, or like the Celtic Cernunnos, who was fully human but had antlers. Medieval myths often had characters that slipped back and forth between human and animal forms almost without comment.

The most important wild animals in Celtic religious imagery were the stag, boar, and wolf, and the most important domestic animals were the bull, horse, and dog. The stag's antlers, boar's tusks, and bull's horns marked their heads as being special, connecting them to the Celtic worship of animal and human heads. The stag and the horse were wild and domestic aspects of agility and speed; the boar and the bull were the wild and domestic aspects of aggression and stamina. The dog was associated with the world of the dead, with healing and the qualities of the warrior, and with the bravery of a wolf. Many Irish warriors had names containing elements meaning "dog" or "wolf." The most famous of these is Cú Chulainn, "the hound of Culainn."

Below: This stone frieze of horses' heads from around the second century BCE was uncovered in a Celtic village in France.

contemporary written evidence to supplement it, the practices of Celtic religion have always been to some extent constructed using educated guesswork.

Another source of information is the myths that were transcribed from Wales and Ireland during medieval times. Many of these stories were first told, and are set, during the ages before Christianity came to Britain and Ireland in the fourth and fifth centuries CE. However, they were first written down by Christian monks, who probably amended the stories to eliminate any pagan material that they found offensive. The stories preserved in the Welsh *Mabinogi* (see box, page 280), a collection of 11 tales that involve characters clearly derived from Celtic mythology, are presented as folktales. The material from southern Ireland is more extensive and includes stories such as *Lebor Gab la Eerenn* or "The Book of Invasions," "The Battle of Moytura," and "The Wooing of Étain," while the northern Irish Ulster cycle of tales, which features the hero Cú Chulainn and culminates in "The Cattle Raid of Cooley," also tells of interactions between gods and men.

LESLIE ELLEN JONES

Bibliography

Ellis, Peter Berresford. *Celtic Myths and Legends*. New York: Carroll and Graf, 2002.

Heinz, Sabine. *Symbols of the Celts*. New York: Sterling Publications, 1999.

MacKillop, James. *A Dictionary of Celtic Mythology*. New York: Oxford University Press, 1998.

SEE ALSO: Animal-headed Figures; Animals; Calendars; Druids; Nature Religions; Rome; Sacrifice.

INDEX

Page numbers in *italics* refer to picture captions. Page numbers in **bold** refer to main articles.